Kids'
Fun & Healthy
COOKBOOK

Senior Editor Catherine Saunders
Senior Designer Lisa Crowe
Canadian Editor Barbara Campbell
Editor Julia March, Alisha Niehaus
Editorial Assistant Elizabeth Noble
Designers Thelma-Jane Robb and Dan Bunyan
DTP Designer Hanna Ländin
Home Economist Denise Smart
Publishing Manager Simon Beecroft
Category Publisher Alex Allan/Siobhan Williamson
Production Amy Bennett

First Canadian edition, 2020
DK Canada
320 Front Street West, Suite 1400
Toronto, Ontario M5V 3B6

Library and Archives Canada Cataloguing in Publication
Title: Kids' fun & healthy cookbook / written by Nicola Graimes ; photography by Howard Shooter.
Other titles: Kids' fun and healthy cookbook
Names: Graimes, Nicola, author. | Shooter, Howard, photographer.
Description: Canadian edition. | Includes index.
Identifiers: Canadiana 20190080655 | ISBN 9781553633044 (softcover)
Subjects: LCSH: Cooking—Juvenile literature. | LCGFT: Cookbooks.
Classification: LCC TX652.5 .G73 2020 | DDC j641.5/123—dc23

DK books are available at special discounts when purchased in bulk for corporate sales, sales promotions,
premiums, fund-raising, or educational use. For details, please contact specialmarkets@dk.com

Reproduced by Media Development and Printing Ltd., UK
Printed and bound in China

Acknowledgements
The publisher would like to thank the following for their kind permission to reproduce their photographs:
(Key: a-above; b-below/bottom; c-centre; f-far; l-left; r-right; t-top)
Cover images: Front: **123RF.com:** Elena Shashkina c; Spine: **123RF.com:** Elena Shashkina
Interior images: p.56 tl: © All Rights Reserved: *Canada's Food Guide.* **Health Canada.** Adapted and reproduced
with permission from the Minister of Health, 2020.

All other images © Dorling Kindersley
For further information see: www.dkimages.com

The publisher would like to thank the photographer's assistants Jon Cardwell and Michael Hart for all their help,
and the following young chefs for working so hard to make this book so fun *and* healthy:
Efia Brady, Ella Bukbardis, Megan Craddock, Eliza Greenslade, George Greenslade, Eva Mee, Grace Mee,
Shannon O'Kelly, Gabriella Soper, Rachel Tilley, Charlotte Vogel, and Hope Wadman.

A WORLD OF IDEAS:
SEE ALL THERE IS TO KNOW

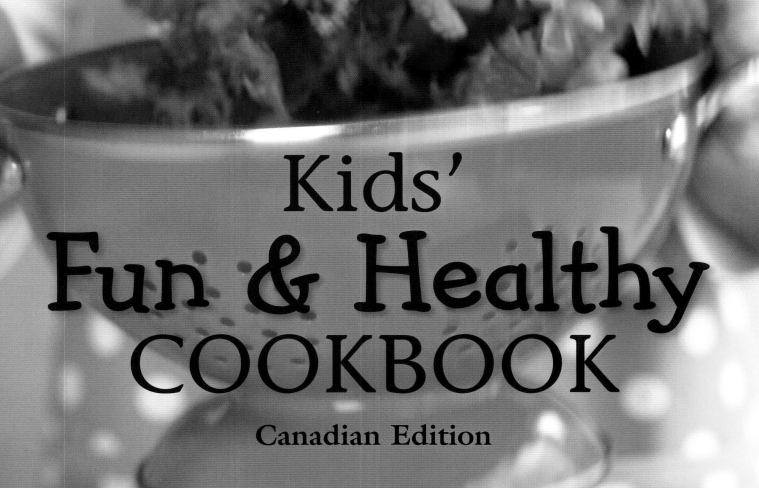

Kids'
Fun & Healthy
COOKBOOK

Canadian Edition

Written by Nicola Graimes
Photography by Howard Shooter

DK

Contents

Baked Potato
See p.35

Strawberry Yogourt Crunch
See p.24–25

Fruit Yogourt
See p.86

Italian Tuna Pasta
See p.58–59

Baking

Desserts

Glossary

Index

Sunflower Seed Rolls
See p.122–123

Introduction

In this book you'll find out why healthy eating is important and how to make your diet balanced *and* tasty. You will also discover lots of ideas for balanced breakfasts, luscious light meals, and mouthwatering main meals, all designed to suit even the pickiest eaters. And don't worry, there are plenty of recipes for desserts, cakes, and cookies—but with a healthy twist!

Getting started

1. Read the recipe thoroughly before you begin.

2. Wash your hands, tie your hair back (if necessary), and put on your apron.

3. Gather all the ingredients and equipment you need before you begin.

4. Start cooking!

Be sensible! Take extra care when you see this symbol, because hot ovens, burners, or sharp knives are involved.

You might need to ask an adult for help if you see this symbol. But don't be shy—ask for help whenever you think you need it!

Why learn to cook?

Cooking is great fun—but more importantly it is a fantastic skill that will be useful to you for the rest of your life. If you know how to cook, you can always feed yourself along with your family and friends! In addition, you will also know exactly what is going into your food, which means that you can make healthier choices than when you eat ready-made meals or fast food.

Making food to share with family and friends is also a great way to spend time with the people you care about. When you take the time to cook and eat with others, it can be the perfect opportunity to catch up, talk about your day, and to share experiences. Why not ask your parents, grandparents, or other family members to teach you special family recipes?

Safe cooking

Cooking involves heat and sharp objects, so you must take care to be safe and sensible.

- Use oven mitts when handling hot items.
- Don't put hot pans or trays directly onto the work surface—use a heatproof trivet, mat, rack, or board.
- When you are stirring food on the burner, grip the handle firmly to steady the pan.
- When cooking on the stove, turn pan handles to the side (away from the heat and the front) so that you are less likely to knock them over.
- Take extra care on any step where you see the red warning triangle.
- Ask an adult for help when you see the green warning triangle.

Kitchen hygiene

After safety, cleanliness is the most important thing to be aware of in the kitchen. Here are a few simple hygiene rules for you to follow.

- Always wash your hands before you start cooking and after handling raw meat.
- Wash all fruits and vegetables.
- Use separate cutting boards for meat and vegetables, and wash them well after using.
- Keep your cooking area clean and have a cloth or paper towel handy to wipe up any spills.
- Store cooked and raw food separately.
- Always check the best-before date on all ingredients. Do not use them if the date has passed.
- Keep meat and fish in the refrigerator until you need them and always cook them thoroughly.

Using the recipes

The recipes don't just tell you how to cook food, they suggest alternatives, give helpful advice, and provide some amazing facts about the food you eat. In Canada, we use the metric system for measurements, but some people still use imperial measurements while cooking, such as cups and teaspoons, and many ovens in Canada are set to give the temperature in Fahrenheit (so make sure to check your oven's settings and use Fahrenheit if this is the case). Both metric and imperial measurements are included in the recipes so you can choose the method that suits you.

Check here for preparation and cooking times.

All the recipes can be adapted to suit your personal taste.

Collect all the ingredients and equipment you need before you start.

Step-by-step pictures and text guide you through the recipes.

This tells you which section the recipe is from.

Discover some amazing food trivia in this box.

Check out useful cooking tips.

Learn more about why certain foods are good for you.

Fruits and Vegetables

Eating lots of fruits and vegetables is a vital part of a healthy diet, and some scientists believe it could actually help you to live longer. Fresh fruits and vegetables may even help to protect you against many of the major diseases found in the modern world, including cancer and heart disease.

Canada's Food Guide recommends that you should fill at least half of your plate with different fruits and vegetables for every meal. Eat a wide variety of fruits and vegetables to get the most benefit. See page 56 for an image of the ideal balance of the different food groups.

Why are fruits and vegetables good for you?

Fruits and vegetables are good for you because they provide important vitamins, minerals, fibre, and natural plant compounds known as phytochemicals. As well as their health benefits, these phytochemicals are responsible for the colour, taste, and smell of a fruit or vegetable.

What doesn't count?

There are a few foods that shouldn't count towards your daily amount of fruits and vegetables, because they do not have a high enough real fruit or vegetable content. These are:

- Ketchup and the tomato sauce in beans (although the beans do count towards your daily protein amount)
- Fruit-flavoured drinks, such as Kool-Aid
- Store-bought fruit yogourts
- Jam, marmalade, or jelly

Remember: fresh and unprocessed is best!

Melon Fruit Bowl
p.88–89

I can eat a rainbow...

Fruits and vegetables are a colourful and fun part of any healthy, balanced diet. Different-coloured fruits and vegetables provide different nutrients.

Red

Red fruits and vegetables such as tomatoes, bell peppers, strawberries, grapes, and cherries are a great source of vitamin C, which supports the immune system and helps the condition of your skin, hair, and nails.

tomatoes

Yellow

The yellow colour of fruits and vegetables such as bananas, bell peppers, corn, melon, and pineapple comes from carotenoids, which have been found to protect the body against cancer and heart disease.

yellow peppers

Orange

Orange fruits and vegetables such as carrots, pumpkin, squash, mango, apricots, and bell peppers contain large amounts of beta-carotene and vitamin C. Beta-carotene is great for boosting your immune system and research shows that vitamin C can significantly reduce the length and severity of a cold. If you haven't already, give pumpkin and squash a try because they contain even more beta-carotene than large carrot!

oranges

Green

Broccoli, cabbage, and sprouts have all been described as super-vegetables because they are so rich in vitamins and minerals, particularly beta-carotene, vitamins B and C, iron, potassium, and calcium that help to support your immune system.

broccoli

Did you know?

It can be difficult to get the right balance but you won't go wrong if you eat a combination of different coloured fruits and vegetables every day—they can be fresh, frozen, canned, or dried.

Purple

Purple fruits and vegetables, such as grapes, eggplants, black currants, blueberries, blackberries, figs, beets, and red cabbage are an excellent source of vitamin C. They also contain bioflavonoids, which help your body to absorb vitamin C and reduce pain if you bump or bruise yourself.

blueberries

Whole Grains and other carbohydrates

Rice, pasta, cereals, and bread can all be good sources of whole grains and carbohydrates. These foods are a main source of energy for the body, and also contain useful amounts of fibre, vitamins and, perhaps surprisingly, protein. Potatoes are also a type of carbohydrate, as are sugary foods (see pp.14–15).

About a quarter of your plate should be filled with whole grain foods (see p.56). Choices include whole wheat pasta, brown rice, whole grain bread, and breakfast cereals made with whole grains.

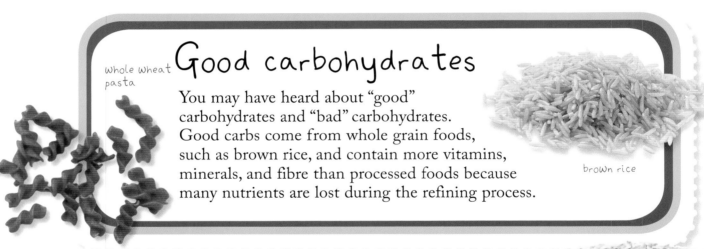

Good carbohydrates

whole wheat pasta

You may have heard about "good" carbohydrates and "bad" carbohydrates. Good carbs come from whole grain foods, such as brown rice, and contain more vitamins, minerals, and fibre than processed foods because many nutrients are lost during the refining process.

brown rice

Bread

The best types of bread are those made from whole wheat flour, as they provide B vitamins, vitamin E, and fibre. White bread still has some vitamins and minerals but is lacking in fibre. There are plenty of interesting varieties to choose from, including:

- **Tortilla**
- **Pita**
- **Bagels**
- **Soda bread**
- **Rye bread**
- **Foccacia**
- **Ciabatta**

Oat Bread see p.106

Grains and cereals

Grains have been grown throughout the world for centuries. These seeds of cereal grasses are very versatile and also low in fat:

- **Wheat**
- **Rye**
- **Quinoa**
- **Millet**
- **Buckwheat**
- **Couscous**

- **Bulgur wheat**
- **Oats**
- **Barley**
- **Farro**

Breakfast cereal see p.16

Rice

Rice is popular in many countries throughout the world and forms an important part of diets in India, China, and Japan. There are many types to choose from:

- **Long-grain**
- **Short-grain (rice pudding)**
- **Basmati**
- **Arborio (risotto)**
- **Sticky rice (sushi)**

Jambalaya see p.76–77

Fibre

Whole grain foods are also a good source of dietary fibre, which is only found in foods that come from plants. High fibre foods include whole wheat bread, brown rice, whole wheat pasta, and whole grain breakfast cereals, which mostly contain insoluble fibre. Although the body cannot digest this type of fibre, it helps the passage of other food and waste products through your gut and keeps your bowels working properly. Soluble fibre is found in oats and beans and can be digested by your body.

oats

Potatoes

There are thousands of potato varieties and certain types are best suited to particular cooking methods, such as roasting, boiling, or mashing. Vitamins and minerals are found in—or just below—the skin, so it is best to serve potatoes unpeeled or scrubbed. The skin is also the best source of fibre.

potatoes

Protein

About a quarter of your plate should be filled with protein (see p.56). Canada's Food Guide recommends choosing more plant proteins than animal proteins.

There are lots of different types of foods in this group, and protein is found in both animal and plant sources. Protein is made up of amino acids, which are essential for building you up and keeping you strong. Try to get your protein from a wide range of foods, including both animal and plant sources.

Lamb Kebabs
See p. 68–69

Meat

Meat is a good source of vitamins and minerals such as iron, zinc, selenium, and B vitamins, but it can also be high in saturated fat (see p.14–15). It is best to choose lean cuts of meat or cut off excess fat before cooking. Poultry is lower in fat than red meat, especially if the skin is removed.

Types of red meat:
- Beef
- Pork
- Lamb
- Venison

Types of poultry:
- Chicken
- Turkey
- Duck
- Game hen

Tofu and eggs are two valuable sources of protein. Tofu also provides calcium, iron, and vitamins B1, B2, and B3 (see p.48–49 and 78–79), while eggs contain B vitamins, iron, calcium, and zinc.

tofu

Nuts and seeds

Nuts and seeds are a good source of protein and also provide a rich collection of vitamins, minerals, and healthy fats such as omega-6 (see p.14–15). However, because they are high in fat, you should try not to eat too many—and you should also try to avoid salted nuts.

Types of nuts and seeds:
- Peanuts
- Brazil nuts
- Walnuts
- Cashews
- Hazelnuts
- Almonds
- Sunflower seeds
- Sesame seeds
- Pumpkin seeds
- Poppy seeds
- Flax seeds

Fish

You should eat at least two portions of fish a week, including one of oily fish. Salmon, tuna, sardines, mackerel, trout, and herring are all types of oily fish that are rich in omega-3 fats (see p.14–15,) as well as protein.

Salmon Parcels
see p.70–71

Legumes

Legumes include beans, peas, and lentils. As well as being a good source of protein, they are low in fat and also contain fibre, B vitamins, and good carbohydrates. Canned legumes are quick and easy to use, but try to buy products without added sugar and salt.

Popular legumes:
- Lentils
- Dried peas
- Chick peas
- Black-eyed peas
- Pinto beans
- Cannellini beans
- Kidney beans
- Soy beans

Did you know?

A fried chicken breast contains nearly 6 times as much fat as a grilled, skinless chicken breast.

milk

Dairy

As well as protein, dairy products provide valuable vitamins and minerals, such as calcium and vitamins A, B12, and D.

Yogourt Swirl with Dippers
see p. 26–27

Types of dairy
- Milk
- Yogourt
- Cheese
- Butter
- Cottage cheese
- Cream
- Crème fraîche
- Buttermilk
- Kefir

Alternatives to dairy
- Fortified breakfast cereals
- Soy or almond milk
- Tofu
- Green leafy vegetables
- Molasses
- Canned salmon
- Baked beans
- Sea vegetables
- Sesame seeds

For strong bones and teeth, eat 2–3 servings of calcium-rich foods a day. A serving equals a glass of milk, a small container of yogourt, or a small portion of cheese.

Fats and Sugars

You need some fat in your diet because it provides your body with lots of energy, helps it to absorb some vitamins, and provides essential fatty acids, such as omega-3 and omega-6. But it is important to eat the right types, such as polyunsaturated and monounsaturated, and to try and avoid saturated and trans fats.

Be careful not to eat too much fat. A good way to check how much fat your food contains is to look at the label. 20 g (¾ oz) of fat per 100 g (3½ oz) of food is a lot of fat; and 3 g (1/10 oz) or less of fat per 100 g (3½ oz) is a little fat. Use what you learn in this book to be sensible about your fat intake.

fries

croissants

cheese

Unhealthy fats

Saturated and trans fats are generally solid at room temperature and are primarily from animal sources (except fish). They are found in lard, butter, hard margarine, cheese, whole-fat milk, and anything that contains these ingredients, such as cakes, chocolate, cookies, pies, and pastries. Saturated fat is also the white fat you can see on red meat and underneath poultry skin. The less saturated fat you eat, the better it is for your health—a high fat intake has been linked with an increased risk of coronary heart disease.

cake

avocadoes

olive oil

Healthy fats

Unsaturated fats—polyunsaturated and monounsaturated—are usually liquid at room temperature. They are a much healthier alternative to saturated fat, helping to fuel the body, transport nutrients around the body, and also to protect your heart. Unsaturated fats generally come from vegetable sources (and some fish). These sources include vegetable oils such as sesame, sunflower, soy, and olive; plus nuts, seeds, avocadoes, and oily fish, such as mackerel, sardines, and salmon. However, although these fats are healthy you only need a small amount to get the health benefits you need.

sunflower seeds

hazelnuts

fish

Some simple ways to cut down on unhealthy fats

- Snack on unsalted nuts and seeds instead of cookies and chips.
- Spread mashed avocado or hummus on toast, instead of butter.
- Choose oily fish instead of breaded and fried fish.
- For a change, mash olive oil into potatoes instead of butter.
- Drizzle olive oil and lemon juice over salads in place of creamy salad dressings.
- Nibble fresh or dried fruit rather than cookies and chocolate.
- Trim any visible fat off meat and poultry.
- Buy lean cuts of meat.
- Ditch the frying pan—try poaching, steaming, broiling, or baking.
- Swap whole-fat milk for low-fat or fat-free alternatives.
- If you use lard, butter, or margarine, switch to plant-based oils and low-fat spreads.

raisins

raspberries

strawberries

hummus

Sugary foods

jam

Like fat, sugar is a concentrated source of energy. It is found in foods such as jam, sweets, cakes, chocolate, Kool-Aid, cookies, and ice cream. The psychological benefits of eating these foods are obvious— they taste delicious! However, too much sugar causes tooth decay, obesity, and mood swings so it is important to limit your intake.

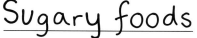

lollipops

soda

Salt

chips

Eating too much salt is linked to high blood pressure, heart disease, and strokes. It's not just obvious foods such as chips and salted peanuts that contain salt; it is also hiding in breakfast cereals, bread, cakes, and cookies. This means that it can be very difficult to tell if you are eating too much, so check your food labels first to see if salt has been added. When it comes to adding salt at the dinner table, it is easy to get into the habit of using too much. Always taste your food before reaching for the salt—you may find your food tastes fine without it.

salt

Breakfasts

After a night's sleep you need fuel—a good breakfast to prepare you for the day ahead. Foods high in carbohydrates, such as cereals and bread, are ideal breakfast foods because they are broken down into glucose which fuels your brain. Protein foods such as yogourt, milk, eggs, sausages, bacon, and beans are important, too. They control the growth and development of the body, and boost alertness. There are lots of tasty recipes in this section, but these ideas will get you started.

Boiled Egg
Half-fill a small saucepan with water. Gently lower an egg into the pan and bring the water to a boil. Boil the egg for 4 minutes, then remove it with a slotted spoon. Dip it in cold water and place it in an egg cup. Carefully slice the top off the egg and serve with toast.

Naturally Sweet
Store-bought cereals can be very high in sugar. Buy sugar-free wheat or oat flakes instead, and add your favourite combination of dried fruits, nuts, or seeds.

Quick and Easy
Give energy levels a quick boost. Simply add sliced banana, a dollop of natural yogourt, and a drizzle of honey to whole wheat seedy toast or fruit bread.

Add Fruit!
Start the day in a super-healthy way by adding fresh fruit to your breakfast cereal. It provides vitamins and natural sweetness.

Stewed Apple (serves 4)

Peel and core 4 apples, then chop them into bite-sized pieces. Put them into a saucepan and add 5 mL (1 tsp) ground cinnamon, 60 mL (4 tbsp) apple juice, and a squeeze of lemon juice. Half-cover the pan and simmer for 15–20 minutes or until the apples are tender. Serve with a raisin English muffin.

Cooked Breakfast

Treat yourself to a cooked breakfast once in a while, but grill instead of fry it. Use lean meat or vegetarian sausages and add grilled tomatoes, mushrooms, whole wheat toast, and scrambled eggs for a balanced breakfast.

Poached Egg

Fill a pan with water (about 5 cm deep) and bring it to a simmer. Crack an egg into a cup. Swirl the water in the pan and then gently pour the egg into the centre of the pan. Cook for 3 minutes or until the white is set and the yolk is slightly runny. Scoop out using a slotted spoon and serve with whole wheat toast.

Oatmeal (serves 4)

Put 250 mL (1 cup) oats in a saucepan with 325 mL (1⅓ cups) milk and 250 mL (1 cup) water. Bring to a boil, then reduce the heat and simmer, stirring, for about 4 minutes or until creamy and smooth.

Fruit Salad

Fruit salads are perfect for breakfast, dessert, or as a healthy snack. Use a combination of your favourite fruits. Yogourt also tastes great with this recipe.

Boost Nutrients

A sprinkling of seeds or chopped nuts will boost the nutritional content of oatmeal and other breakfast cereals as well as adding extra flavour.

Carrot and Apple Juice

This fresh juice is bursting with vitamin C! Don't worry if you don't have a juicer—just remove the apple cores and make a purée using a blender or food processor. Then use a sieve to separate the juice from the pulp.

For maximum goodness, drink the juice immediately.

Healthy Hint

The lemon helps to preserve the vitamins in the juice and also brings out the flavour of the apple and carrot.

Ingredients

- 4 apples
- 3 carrots
- squeeze of fresh lemon juice (optional)

Equipment

- small sharp knife
- cutting board
- juicer

juicer

1 Scrub the carrots and cut each one into 2 or 3 pieces. Remove the stems from the apples and carefully cut them into quarters.

2 Put the apples and carrots through the juicer. Throw away the pulp and pour the juice into two glasses. Add a squeeze of lemon and stir the juice.

Fruit Smoothie

This creamy drink will give you plenty of energy for the day ahead—and it's so easy to make! Serve it with cereal or toast for a complete breakfast.

Tasty Twist

Swap the blueberries with the same amount of strawberries for a classic combination.

Ingredients

- 175 mL (¾ cup) fresh or frozen blueberries
- 3 bananas (sliced)
- 5 mL (1 tsp) vanilla extract (optional)
- 500 mL (2 cups) thick plain yogourt
- 250 mL (1 cup) milk

banana   blueberries

Equipment

- small sharp knife
- cutting board
- blender

cutting board

1 Peel the bananas and then roughly chop them into small slices. Put them into the blender and add the blueberries, vanilla extract, yogourt, and milk.

2 Whiz in the blender until the mixture is smooth, thick, and creamy. Pour the smoothie into four tall glasses and enjoy this simple and nutritious breakfast.

Fruit and Nut Bars

This homemade version of a fruit cereal bar is packed with energy-giving apricots, raisins, nuts, and seeds. It makes an excellent start to the day, especially with a calcium-rich glass of milk or cup of yogourt. It could also be a healthy addition to a lunchbox.

Tasty Twists

Any type of dried fruit or nuts can be used to make these bars. You can experiment with pre-mixed bags, but be sure to check the amount of salt added.

Ingredients

- 75 mL (⅓ cup) hazelnuts
- 150 mL (⅔ cup) whole oats
- 175 mL (¾ cup) raisins
- 250 mL (1 cup) dried apricots (cut into small pieces)
- 60 mL (4 tbsp) orange juice
- 30 mL (2 tbsp) sunflower seeds
- 30 mL (2 tbsp) pumpkin seeds

raisins

pumpkin seeds

sunflower seeds

oats

Equipment

- frying pan
- spatula
- small sharp knife
- cutting board
- food processor or blender
- large mixing bowl
- parchment paper
- 18 cm x 25 cm pan

spatula

1 Put the hazelnuts, oats, and seeds into a frying pan. Toast (stirring) over a medium heat for 3 mins, or until they begin to turn golden. Leave to cool.

2 Put the raisins, apricots, and orange juice into a food processor and purée until the mixture becomes smooth. Pour the purée into a mixing bowl.

3 Put the nuts, oats, and seeds in the food processor and whiz until they are finely chopped. Pour the mixture into the bowl with the fruit purée.

Cut into 8–10 slices and eat as part of a nutritious breakfast.

Did you know?

Hazelnuts are high in fibre, potassium, calcium, magnesium, and vitamin E, so they are nutritious as well as tasty!

4 Stir the fruit mixture until all the ingredients are mixed together. Line a 18 cm x 25 cm baking pan with parchment paper.

5 Spread the mixture evenly in the pan. Chill for at least 1 hour, until solid. Then turn it out of the tin and peel off the parchment paper. Cut into bars.

Food Facts

Drying fruit is one of the oldest methods of preserving it. The drying process concentrates nutrients, making dried fruit a useful source of fibre, natural sugars, vitamins B and C, iron, calcium, and other minerals. However, levels of vitamin C in dried fruit are lower than if it's fresh!

dried apricots

Mixed Fruit Crackle

Store-bought cereals can be full of unnecessary sugar. This healthier version relies on the natural sweetness of the dried fruit, which is also full of fibre and nutrients such as iron. Just add milk for a delicious and nutritious breakfast!

Tasty Twists

Any mixture of your favourite fruits and nuts can be used in this recipe. For a different texture, you could swap the puffed rice for oats to make muesli. Or try serving the cereal with a tasty topping of fresh fruit.

Ingredients

hazelnuts

- 125 mL (½ cup) whole hazelnuts
- 120 mL (8 tbsp) sunflower seeds
- 250 mL (1 cup) dried apricots (cut into small pieces)
- 2.25 L (10 cups) sugar-free puffed rice cereal   *puffed rice cereal*
- 250 mL (1 cup) raisins
- 150 mL (⅔ cup) flaked coconut

dried apricots

Equipment

- frying pan
- wooden spoon
- small bowl
- freezer bag
- rolling pin
- kitchen scissors
- mixing bowl

rolling pin

frying pan

Did you know?

The average North American eats 4.5 kilograms (10 lbs) of cereal a year—that's about 160 bowls!

1 Put the nuts in a frying pan and toast over a medium-low heat. Turn the nuts using a wooden spoon and cook for 3 minutes or until they begin to turn golden.

2 Pour the nuts into a bowl and leave them to cool. Put the sunflower seeds in the frying pan and fry for 2 minutes. They should turn golden but not burned.

3 Leave the sunflower seeds to cool. Pour the cooled nuts into a small plastic bag. Fold over the open end and hold it closed with one hand.

Storing the cereal in an airtight container will keep it fresh for longer.

Food Facts

Nuts and seeds provide a nutritious combination of B vitamins, iron, vitamin E, and zinc, plus omega-6 fats, which are important for brain function and energy levels. Sunflower seeds help to keep your immune system strong as they provide zinc, magnesium, and selenium. Their vitamin E content helps to keep skin healthy.

sunflower seeds

4 Using your other hand, bash the nuts with the rolling pin until they are broken into small pieces. Then cut the apricots into small pieces.

5 Put the puffed rice cereal into a large mixing bowl. Add the apricots, nuts, seeds, raisins, and coconut and gently mix together with your hands.

10 mins ● **Cooking** 5 mins ● **Serves** 2

Strawberry Yogourt Crunch

Toasted oats and seeds make this layered breakfast a crunchy treat, and provide important nutrients too. The yogourt is a low-fat source of protein and calcium, while the strawberries and orange juice are rich in vitamin C. Honey adds natural sweetness, but you could use maple syrup instead.

Tasty Twists

Swap strawberries for your favourite fruits such as bananas, nectarines, or peaches. Fruit purée also tastes great! (See p.26–27 and 86.)

Ingredients

- 250 mL (1 cup) whole strawberries (about 6-8)
- 60 mL (4 tbsp) orange juice
- 150 mL (⅔ cup) whole oats
- 45 mL (3 tbsp) sunflower seeds
- 45 mL (3 tbsp) pumpkin seeds
- 30–45 mL (2-3 tbsp) clear runny honey
- 60 mL (4 tbsp) thick plain yogourt

honey

pumpkin seeds

strawberries

Equipment

- small sharp knife
- cutting board
- small bowl
- frying pan
- wooden spoon

cutting board

1 Cut the stems and leaves from the strawberries and then thickly slice the fruit. Put the strawberries in a bowl and add the orange juice. Set aside.

2 Put the oats in a frying pan and toast over a medium-low heat for 3 mins, turning the oats occasionally with a wooden spoon to make sure they cook evenly.

3 Add the sunflower and pumpkin seeds and toast for another 2 minutes or until light golden. Take care—the pumpkin seeds may pop a little!

This would also be delicious for dessert!

Food Facts

Oats are full of fibre and carbohydrates. They are perfect for breakfast because the fibre in them is digested by the body slowly. This makes you feel full for longer and keeps your blood sugar levels steady. Oats are also a great source of vitamins E, B1, and B2.

oats

4 Take the pan off the heat. Stir in the honey—it will sizzle at first, but keep stirring until the oats and seeds are coated. Allow to cool slightly.

5 Put a layer of the oats in the bottom of each glass. Add 2 heaped spoonfuls of yogourt and then some of the fruit. Add another layer of each.

Yogourt Swirl with Dippers

Unlike many store-bought yogourts, this recipe does not contain any refined sugar or additives. Instead these tasty yogourts are low in fat and high in calcium, protein, and potassium with a swirl of vitamin-rich dried fruit. Have fun dipping the toasted bread fingers into your breakfast!

Tasty Twists

Fresh fruit or fruit purées are also good mixed into yogourt. Try mango, strawberry, raspberry, or stewed apples. (See p.17 and 86.)

Ingredients

- 175 mL (¾ cup) dried dates or apricots (chopped)
- 250 mL (1 cup) water
- 45 mL (3 tbsp) apple juice
- 500 mL (2 cups) thick plain yogourt
- 4–8 slices raisin bread

dried dates

dried apricots

Equipment

- medium saucepan with lid
- blender
- spoon
- 4 bowls

bowl

⚠️

1 Put the dates or apricots and water in the saucepan. Bring to a boil and then reduce the heat to low. Cover, and cook the fruit for 15-20 mins, or until soft.

Fruit muffins or bagels could also be dipped!

Food Facts

Yogourt contains beneficial bacteria that are thought to help boost your immune system, help your digestive system, and fight off infection.

yogourt

Did you know?

Yogourt has been around since ancient times. The word itself originates from the Turkish language.

2 Leave the dates or apricots to cool for about 30 minutes and then stir in the apple juice. Spoon the mixture into a blender and whiz until smooth.

3 Divide the yogourt between four bowls. Put 30 mL (2 tbsp) of the fruit purée on top of each serving and then stir gently to make a swirled pattern.

4 Toast the raisin bread until it is light golden. Cut the toast into narrow strips and dip them into the yogourt mixture. Delicious!

Banana Pancakes

These pancakes make a tasty and nutritious brunch when served with summer berries and a drizzle of maple syrup. Fruit sauce (see p.86) and yogourt would also make delicious toppings.

Helpful Hint

It's important that the batter is free from lumps. If you do get lumps in your batter, press it through a sieve using the back of a spoon.

Ingredients

- 175 mL (¾ cup) self-rising flour
- 75 mL (⅓ cup) self-rising whole wheat flour
- 30 mL (2 tbsp) sugar
- 1 egg
- 175 mL (¾ cup) milk
- 2 bananas (peeled)
- butter (for frying)

whole wheat flour

sieve

egg

Equipment

- sieve
- 2 bowls
- wooden spoon
- measuring cup
- whisk or fork
- large non-stick frying pan
- ladle
- spatula
- fork or masher

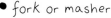
ladle

mixing bowl

1 Sift both types of flour into a mixing bowl, adding any bran left in the sieve. Stir in the sugar and make a well in the centre of the mixture.

2 Pour the milk into a measuring cup and crack the egg straight into it. Lightly beat the egg and milk with a fork or whisk until they are mixed.

Food Facts

Choose ripe bananas when making these pancakes. They are not only easier to mash, but their nutrients—vitamins B and C, potassium, iron, and beta-carotene—are more easily absorbed by the body. Underripe bananas are more difficult to digest and can give you a stomach ache.

bananas

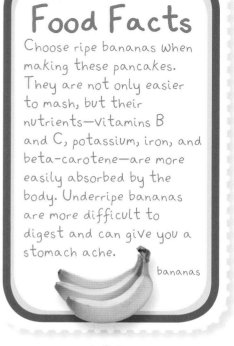

3 Pour the egg mixture into the well in the centre of the flour and sugar. Beat with a wooden spoon until you have a smooth, creamy batter.

4 Leave the batter to rest for about 30 minutes—this will make the pancakes lighter. Mash the bananas in a bowl then stir them into the rested batter.

Did you know?

The French word for pancakes is "crêpes." In Russian they are called "blinis," and in Spanish they are called "panqueques."

5 Heat a small pat of butter in a frying pan. Add 3 small ladlefuls of batter to make 3 pancakes, each one about 8 cm in diameter.

6 Cook for 2 minutes, or until bubbles appear on the surface. Flip the pancakes and cook for another 2 minutes, so both sides are light golden.

7 Keep the cooked pancakes warm in a low oven while you cook more pancakes with the rest of the batter, adding a new pat of butter before each batch.

Eggs in Rolls

Eggs are a great source of high quality protein —ideal for kick-starting your day! This recipe is perfect for a filling weekend brunch or even a light meal.

Helpful Hint

Timing and temperature are really important when cooking scrambled eggs. If they are cooked for too long over too high a heat, the eggs become dry and crumbly.

Did you know?

The type of hen determines the colour of the egg shell. Those with white feathers and earlobes lay white eggs and those with red feathers and earlobes lay brown eggs.

Ingredients

- 4 crusty rolls
- 3 tomatoes (optional)
- 8 eggs
- 75 mL (5 tbsp) milk
- salt and pepper
- 52 mL (3½ tbsp) unsalted butter

crusty rolls

tomatoes

Equipment

whisk

- sharp knife
- cutting board
- mixing bowl
- whisk or fork
- medium saucepan
- spoon

cutting board

1 Slice the tops off the rolls and then use your fingers to scoop out the centre of each one. (The insides can be used to make breadcrumbs.)

2 Cut the tomatoes in half and scoop out the seeds with a spoon. Then slice the de-seeded tomatoes into small, bite-sized pieces.

Food Facts

Eggs are one of the most nutritious foods and make a valuable contribution to your diet. They contain B vitamins, iron, calcium, and zinc, as well as protein. However, four eggs per week is the maximum recommended intake, as they are high in cholesterol. The eggs of many different types of birds can be eaten, but those of the female chicken (hen) are most widely available.

eggs

3 Crack each egg into a mixing bowl by tapping it firmly against the side, pushing your thumbs into the crack, and pulling the shell apart.

4 Add the milk to the bowl. Whisk the eggs and milk together using a fork or small hand whisk. Season the mixture with a little salt and pepper.

5 Put the butter into the saucepan and melt it over medium to low heat. When the butter begins to bubble, add the tomatoes and cook for 1 minute.

6 Pour in the egg mixture. Stir gently to prevent the egg from sticking to the pan. Continue for 3 minutes or until the eggs are firm. Remove from the heat.

7 Spoon a serving of scrambled egg and tomatoes into each roll. Balance the roll lids on top and serve. A glass of orange juice is the perfect accompaniment.

Breakfast Tortilla

A tortilla is a thick, flat omelette and is a popular dish in Spain. This is a twist on the classic combination of eggs, onion, and potatoes and makes a filling breakfast or perfect after-school snack.

Did you know?
"Tortilla" is the Spanish word for omelette. In Italy it is called "frittata." However, in Mexico, "tortilla" means a thin (unleavened) bread, usually made from corn.

Ingredients

eggs

- 4 good-quality sausages (or vegetarian alternative)
- 4 medium-sized potatoes (peeled, cooked, and left to cool)
- 30 mL (2 tbsp) sunflower oil
- 8 cherry tomatoes (halved)
- 5 eggs (lightly beaten)
- salt and pepper

potatoes

cherry tomatoes

Equipment

- foil
- tongs
- cutting board
- medium frying pan
- spatula or wooden spoon
- measuring cup
- whisk or fork
- small sharp knife

frying pan

spatula

1 Preheat your oven broiler. Line a baking pan or sheet with foil and broil the sausages for 10-15 mins, or until cooked through and golden brown.

2 While the sausages are cooling slightly, cut the cooked potatoes into bite-sized chunks. Then cut the cooled sausages into 2.5 cm pieces.

Food Facts

The healthiest sausages are called "lean" and contain much less fat and fewer additives than poor-quality sausages. Turkey and chicken sausages usually have a lower fat content than those made from red meats.

sausages

Tasty Twists

Vegetarian sausages, lean bacon, or cooked chicken would also taste great in this tortilla. Other vegetables such as mushrooms, peppers, or asparagus could also be added.

3 Heat the oil in a frying pan. Add the potatoes and fry them over medium heat for 8 minutes or until golden. Add the tomatoes and cook for 2 mins.

4 Crack the eggs into a measuring cup and beat them together. Season the beaten eggs with salt and pepper. Add the sausages to the frying pan.

5 Add a little more oil to the frying pan if necessary. Pour the eggs into the pan and cook, without stirring, for 5 minutes until the base of the tortilla is set.

6 To cook the top of the tortilla, carefully place the pan under the broiler and cook for another 3–5 minutes, or until the top is set.

7 Carefully remove the pan from the broiler and leave to cool slightly before sliding the tortilla on to a serving plate. Cut into wedges and serve.

Light Meals

It's important to keep energy levels up throughout the day. Regular meals are essential, but topping them off with a couple of healthy snacks will help to give concentration and memory a boost. There are plenty of recipes for delicious and nutritious light meals and snacks to choose from in this section, but here are some more to try!

Veggie Burgers

Put 125 mL (½ cup) canned kidney beans (drained), 1 small onion (chopped), 1 carrot, 125 mL (½ cup) whole wheat breadcrumbs, 15 mL (1 tbsp) peanut butter (optional) and 1 egg into a food processor. Process to a coarse purée, season and chill the mixture for 1 hour. Form into 4 burgers and dust each one in flour. Brush with oil and grill for 5–6 minutes on each side.

Crudités

Most vegetables are better for you when they are raw. Try dipping strips of raw vegetables such as celery, peppers, carrots, or cucumber into hummus or guacamole.

Hummus

Blend 1 x 540 mL (18 oz) can chick peas (drained), 2 garlic cloves (peeled), 30 mL (2 tbsp) sesame seed paste (tahini), the juice of 1 lemon, and 60 mL (4 tbsp) olive oil until smooth and creamy.

Toast Toppings

Mash ½ ripe avocado then spread it thickly on top of whole wheat toast. Hummus or peanut butter taste great on toast, too!

Simply Souper!

Boost the nutritional content of store-bought soups by adding canned beans, cooked lentils, or extra vegetables.

Coleslaw

Add ½ finely shredded small white or red cabbage, 2 grated carrots, 1 grated apple, and 2 chopped green onions to a bowl. Mix together 30 mL (2 tbsp) olive oil, 15 mL (1 tbsp) lemon juice, and 60 mL (4 tbsp) mayonnaise and add to cabbage mixture.

Burger Relish

Roughly chop 4 tomatoes, 1 large apple (peeled and cored), and 1 onion. Place them in a saucepan with 75 mL (⅓ cup) white wine vinegar and 50 mL (¼ cup) sugar. Bring to a boil, then reduce the heat, cover, and simmer for 15 minutes. Uncover the pan and cook for another 20 minutes, or until soft. Purée if you prefer a smooth relish.

Nut Butter

Place 125 mL (½ cup) shelled nuts, such as peanuts or cashews, in a dry frying pan. Toast them for 2–3 minutes over a medium-low heat, until light golden. (Stir frequently to prevent burning.) Put the nuts in a food processor and process until finely chopped. Pour in 45–60 mL (3–4 tbsp) sunflower oil and process to a coarse paste. Store in an airtight jar.

Miso Soup

Miso is made from fermented soy beans and is usually bought in dried or paste form. For a more filling soup, add water plus cooked egg noodles and thin slices of green onion, carrot, and red pepper.

Baked Potato

Preheat an oven to 200°C (400°F). Scrub the potatoes and prick with a fork or insert a skewer through the middle. Bake for 1–1½ hours, until tender in the centre and the skin is crisp. Serve with a healthy filling such as tuna, corn, and peppers.

Corn Chowder

This recipe will really warm you up on a cold day! Chowder is a special kind of thick soup from New England. Although some chowders include fish, this simple recipe relies on nutritious potatoes, sweet corn, and carrot. It tastes great served with the rolls from p.122–123.

Helpful Hint

If you prefer a chunky soup, leave out step 5. For a smooth soup, blend all the mixture in step 5 until it is creamy.

Ingredients

potatoes

- 1 large onion
- 250 mL (1 cup) fresh, frozen, or canned sweet corn
- 1 large carrot
- 350 g (¾ lb) potatoes
- 15 mL (1 tbsp) sunflower oil

onion

- 3 sprigs thyme (optional)
- 3 sprigs parsley (optional)
- 1 bay leaf
- 1.25 L (5 cups) vegetable stock
- 300 mL (1¼ cups) milk
- salt and pepper

carrot

Equipment

vegetable peeler

- small sharp knife
- vegetable peeler
- cutting board
- large saucepan with lid
- wooden spoon
- blender

wooden spoon

1 Peel and roughly chop the onion. Scrub the carrot and then thinly slice it. Finally, peel the potatoes and cut them into small pieces.

2 Heat the oil in a saucepan. Add the onion and sauté over a medium heat for 8 minutes or until soft and slightly golden. Stir the onion occasionally.

3 Next, add the corn, carrot, potatoes, thyme, parsley, and bay leaf to the onions. Cook for 2 minutes, stirring constantly. Add the stock and bring to a boil.

Season your soup to taste with the salt and pepper.

Tasty Twists

Chunks of smoked fish would add a delicious flavour to this soup. Add the fish in step 4 with the milk and simmer for 5 minutes or until cooked.

4 Reduce the heat to medium-low. Cover with a lid and cook for 15 minutes, stirring occasionally. Add the milk and cook for a further 5 minutes.

5 Scoop out some of the vegetables and blend the rest of the soup until smooth. Return the vegetables and blended soup to the pan and warm through.

Food Facts

Rich in complex carbohydrates, sweet corn is also a good source of vitamins A, B, and C. If you use canned sweet corn instead of fresh, make sure you buy the type without added salt or sugar.

sweet corn

Picnic Salad

This recipe is a simplified version of a traditional Greek salad. You could substitute the feta with any of your favourite cheeses such as cheddar, mozzarella, or brie—and add other ingredients, such as olives, peppers, green onions, and lettuce.

Tasty Twists

Canned beans such as chick peas, cannellini, or cranberry beans are a great alternative to cheese. Tuna, salmon, or shrimp would also taste delicious.

Ingredients

- 2 whole wheat pita breads
- 1 small cucumber
- 12 small tomatoes (quartered)
- ½ red onion (thinly sliced)
- 250 mL (1 cup) feta cheese (cut into chunks)

pita breads

Dressing:
- 45 mL (3 tbsp) olive oil
- 15 mL (1 tbsp) lemon juice or white wine vinegar
- 2 mL (½ tsp) Dijon mustard

onion

tomatoes

cucumber

Equipment

- small sharp knife
- cutting board
- small spoon
- empty, clean jam jar
- mixing bowl
- baking sheet

mixing bowl

sharp knife

1 Preheat the oven to 190°C (375°F). Cut along one side of each pita to open it up. Toast the pita in the oven on a baking sheet until crisp, about 10 mins. Leave to cool.

2 Slice the cucumber in half lengthwise and then scoop out the seeds using a small spoon. Cut the lengths in half and then chop into bite-sized pieces.

3 Put the cucumber, tomatoes, and red onion into a salad bowl. Cut the cooled pita breads into small pieces and add them to the bowl.

This salad also tastes delicious with a sprinkling of chopped fresh mint.

4 To make the dressing, put the olive oil, lemon juice, and mustard into a clean jar. Put the lid on and shake until the ingredients are mixed together.

5 Pour the dressing over the salad. Mix the salad with your clean hands until it is coated in dressing. Finally, scatter over the feta cheese and serve.

Food Facts

True feta cheese is only produced in Greece. Traditionally, it was made from ewes' milk but nowadays it is often made with cows' or goats' milk. Like all cheeses, feta is an excellent source of calcium and protein. However, it is also high in fat so it should be eaten in moderation.

feta cheese

Baked Eggs and Ham

These crust-free pies are so simple to make and taste delicious. Traditional crust is high in fat, so this recipe uses ham as a base instead. Serve with ripe, juicy tomatoes, or crunchy salad. They're perfect for brunch, too.

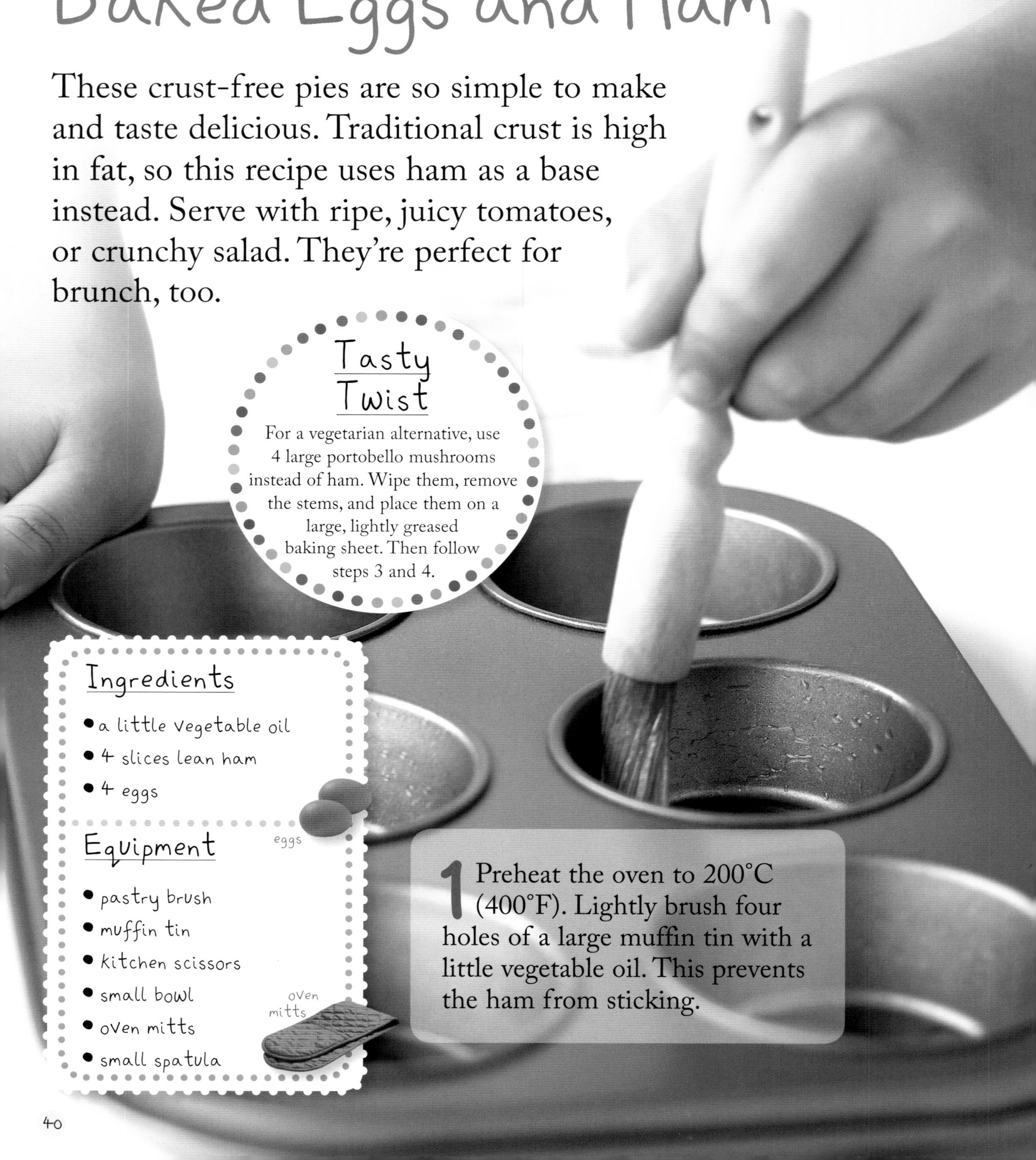

Tasty Twist

For a vegetarian alternative, use 4 large portobello mushrooms instead of ham. Wipe them, remove the stems, and place them on a large, lightly greased baking sheet. Then follow steps 3 and 4.

Ingredients

● a little vegetable oil
● 4 slices lean ham
● 4 eggs

eggs

Equipment

● pastry brush
● muffin tin
● kitchen scissors
● small bowl
● oven mitts
● small spatula

oven mitts

1 Preheat the oven to 200°C (400°F). Lightly brush four holes of a large muffin tin with a little vegetable oil. This prevents the ham from sticking.

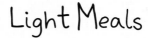

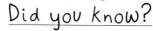

Did you know?

Pies have been around since ancient times. It is believed that the first ever pie recipe was published by the Romans, and it was for rye-crusted goats' cheese and honey pie.

Food Facts

boiled egg

Eggs can be cooked in many different ways. In this recipe, the eggs are baked in the oven until set, but they can also be fried, boiled, scrambled, or poached. To tell if an egg is fresh, place it in a bowl of water—if it sinks and lays flat it is fresh.

2 Arrange a slice of ham in each hole. Carefully trim the slices to make them even, but make sure that the ham is still slightly above the edge of the tin.

3 One by one, crack an egg into a small bowl and pour it into each ham-lined hollow. Bake in the oven for 10–12 minutes, or until the egg has set.

4 Using oven mitts, remove the tray from the oven and leave it to cool for a few minutes. Then carefully lift out the pies with a small spatula.

Tuna Quesadillas and Carrot Salad

Quesadillas are simple to prepare and taste great with a variety of interesting fillings. Best of all, they are delicious hot or cold!

Tasty Twists

For an equally colourful vegetarian alternative, try pesto, sliced tomato, and mozzarella. You could also try the bean filling from p.60–61.

Ingredients

- 2 soft flour tortillas
- ½ can of tuna packed in water (drained)
- 75 mL (⅓ cup) old cheddar (grated)
- 2 green onions (peeled and sliced)

cheddar cheese

- ½ small orange bell pepper (de-seeded and cut into small pieces)
- a little olive oil

green onions

Carrot Salad

- 1 large carrot
- 30 mL (2 tbsp) raisins
- 15 mL (1 tbsp) pine nuts
- 15 mL (1 tbsp) olive oil
- 10 mL (2 tsp) lemon juice

orange bell pepper

Equipment

- spoon
- cutting board
- frying pan
- spatula
- 2 dinner plates
- small sharp knife
- fork
- grater
- 2 mixing bowls

cutting board

frying pan

1 Lay out one of the tortillas on a board or a clean and dry work surface. Leaving a 2 cm border around the edge, spoon the tuna over the top.

2 Sprinkle the cheddar cheese over the tuna and then add the green onions and orange pepper. Place the second tortilla on top and press down firmly.

3 Brush a large frying pan with olive oil. Cook the quesadilla for 2 minutes over medium heat. Press down with a spatula to make sure the cheese melts.

4 Now you need to turn the quesadilla over. Carefully slide it onto a large plate. Put another plate on top and gently turn the plates over.

5 Carefully put the quesadilla back in the pan and cook the other side for 2 minutes. Remove the cooked quesadilla from the pan and cut it into wedges.

Did you know?

Carrots were first grown in Afghanistan in the 7th century. At that time they were red, black, yellow, white, or purple—not orange.

1 Carefully grate the carrot and then put it into a mixing bowl. Add the raisins and pine nuts to the bowl and mix everything together.

2 To make the dressing, mix together the olive oil and lemon juice using a fork. Pour the mixture over the carrot salad and stir to coat the salad evenly.

Colourful Shrimp Salad

Protein, carbohydrates, vitamins, minerals, healthy fats—this salad has it all! In the green corner, avocadoes contain more protein than any other fruit and are also rich in beta-carotene and vitamin E. And in the red corner, tomatoes are good for your immune system and an excellent source of vitamins A, C, and E.

Healthy Hints

If you don't like shrimp or can't get them, cooked chicken is a healthy alternative. Vegetarians could add cooked tofu or pine nuts instead.

Ingredients

- 175 mL (¾ cup) pasta shells
- 250 mL (1 cup) cooked peeled shrimp
- 12 small tomatoes (quartered)
- 1 large avocado
- lettuce leaves (cut into strips)

avocadoes

tomatoes

pasta shells

Dressing:
- 60 mL (4 tbsp) mayonnaise
- 10 mL (2 tsp) lemon juice
- 30 mL (2 tbsp) ketchup
- 2 drops Tabasco sauce (optional)
- salt and pepper

Equipment

- large saucepan
- wooden spoon
- small sharp knife
- cutting board
- mixing bowl
- small bowl
- small spoon

mixing bowl

cutting board

1 Bring a large saucepan of water to a boil. Add the pasta and follow the cooking instructions on the package. Drain well and leave to cool.

2 Carefully cut the avocado around its middle and gently pry it apart. Scoop out the pit with a small spoon and then cut each half into quarters.

3 Peel off the skin and cut the avocado into chunks. Put the avocado into a bowl and spoon half of the lemon juice over it to stop the fruit from turning brown.

Although avocadoes are high in fat, it is the good monounsaturated kind.

Did you know?

Avocadoes were first cultivated in South America. It was believed that a Mayan princess ate the very first avocado and that it held magical powers.

Food Facts

Like all shellfish, shrimp are packed with healthy minerals and are bursting with flavour. Shrimp help to boost the immune system because they contain important minerals called zinc and selenium.

shrimp

4 Put the tomatoes, avocado, and shrimp into a bowl with the pasta, and season. Divide the shredded lettuce leaves between the serving bowls.

5 Mix together all the ingredients for the dressing in a small bowl. Add the shrimp salad to the serving bowls and drizzle the dressing over it.

Minestrone

This wholesome, tasty soup is a version of the traditional Italian soup called minestrone. With the pasta, vegetables, and Parmesan topping it is a complete meal in a bowl!

Minestrone was originally eaten by poor Italians and was made with whatever ingredients were available.

Tasty Twists

You could also add some bacon to the soup, but make sure you cook it thoroughly in step 3. Canned mixed beans, green beans, zucchinis, or peppers would also taste great.

Ingredients

potatoes

- 125 mL (½ cup) pasta bows
- 1 large onion
- 2 potatoes
- 2 sticks celery
- 1 large carrot (scrubbed)
- 15 mL (1 tbsp) olive oil
- 1 bay leaf
- 5 mL (1 tsp) dried oregano
- 1 L (4¼ cups) vegetable stock
- 450 mL (15½ oz) can diced tomatoes
- Parmesan cheese (grated)

carrot

pasta bows

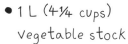

Equipment

- small sharp knife
- cutting board
- medium saucepan
- wooden spoon
- large saucepan with lid
- ladle
- colander

ladle

saucepan

1 Bring a medium-sized pan of water to a boil and add the pasta. Simmer until the pasta is just tender but not completely cooked. Drain well and set aside.

2 Chop the onion into small pieces. Peel the potatoes and cut them into bite-sized chunks. Slice the celery and carrot into bite-sized pieces.

Did you know?

Many people think that Venetian explorer Marco Polo introduced pasta to Italy from China in the 13th century. In fact, pasta has been eaten in Italy since as far back as Roman times!

Helpful Hint

When you drain the pasta in step 1, rinse it with cold water to prevent it sticking together and cooking further.

3 Heat the olive oil in a large saucepan. Add the onion and fry over a medium heat for 8 minutes or until it is softened and golden.

4 Next, add the celery, carrot, potatoes, oregano, and bay leaf. Stir well and pour in the stock and diced tomatoes. Stir again and then bring to a boil.

5 When the soup is bubbling, reduce the heat to low. Half-cover the pan with a lid and simmer the soup for 15 minutes or until the potatoes are tender.

6 Remove the lid, add the pasta, and stir well. Heat the pasta for 5 minutes. Ladle the soup into large bowls and sprinkle with Parmesan cheese.

Food Facts

Pasta is a carbohydrate food and it gives the body energy. Surprisingly, it also provides a small amount of protein. It is best to use whole wheat pasta because it is higher in fibre, vitamins, and minerals than white pasta.

whole wheat pasta

Pita Pockets

Tofu is a very versatile and nutritious ingredient. It naturally has a mild flavour, but when marinated it takes on the flavour of the marinade. The sauce used in this recipe gives the tofu a delicious barbecue taste as well an appetizing golden glow.

Did you know?

Tofu is also known as bean curd. Soy beans are cooked, puréed, and drained to produce a milky liquid. The liquid is mixed with a coagulant to form a custard or cheese-like substance.

Ingredients

tofu

pita breads

- 250 g (9 oz) firm tofu
- a little olive oil
- 3 large lettuce leaves (shredded)
- 2 green onions (peeled and cut into long strips)
- a handful of alfalfa sprouts (optional)

- 4 whole wheat pita breads (warmed in a toaster or oven)

Marinade
- 30 mL (2 tbsp) sweet chili sauce
- 30 mL (2 tbsp) tomato ketchup
- 30 mL (2 tbsp) soy sauce
- 2 mL (½ tsp) ground cumin

Equipment

- paper towel
- small sharp knife
- cutting board
- spoon
- shallow dish
- griddle pan
- spatula or tongs

griddle pan

tongs

1 In a shallow dish, mix together all the ingredients for the marinade. Pat the tofu dry with a paper towel and then cut it into 8 long slices.

2 Put the tofu into the dish with the marinade. Spoon the marinade over the tofu until it is well coated. Leave the tofu to marinate for at least 1 hour.

3 Brush the griddle pan with a generous amount of olive oil and then put it on the heat. Carefully put 4 of the tofu slices into the hot pan.

You could use the marinades from p.74–75 and p.78–79.

Tasty Twists

Strips of chicken, pork, turkey, or beef, or even a medley of vegetables such as pepper, zucchini, and onion make a great alternative to the tofu.

Food Facts

Alfalfa is a seed with a long, slender shoot and a clover-like leaf that is usually bought as a sprouted plant. It is one of the few plant foods that is a complete protein and it is also an excellent source of vitamins B and C.

alfalfa

4 Cook the tofu for 4 minutes on each side, or until golden. As you cook, spoon over more of the marinade. Cook the remaining 4 slices of tofu in the same way.

5 Carefully slice along the edge of the pita breads. Divide the lettuce, green onions, and alfalfa sprouts between the pita breads and then add 2 pieces of tofu.

Griddle Cakes

These savoury sweet-corn pancakes are perfect for a light-but-filling meal or as a tasty brunch on the weekend.

Helpful Hints

Keep the bacon and cooked pancakes warm in the oven while you cook the rest of the griddle cakes. They are delicious served with guacamole.

Did you know?

Corn is a member of the grass family—so it isn't really a vegetable, but a grain. The average ear of corn has 800 kernels, arranged in 16 rows.

Ingredients

whole wheat flour

- 250 mL (1 cup) flour (white or whole wheat)
- 5 mL (1 tsp) baking soda
- 5 mL (1 tsp) baking powder
- 1 egg
- 125 mL (½ cup) milk
- 125 mL (½ cup) sweet corn (fresh, frozen, or canned)
- 300 mL (1¼ cups) buttermilk
- 15 mL (3 tsp) sunflower oil
- 8 bacon strips
- salt and pepper

sweet corn

bacon

Equipment

whisk

- measuring cup
- fork or whisk
- sieve
- large mixing bowl
- wooden spoon
- foil and baking sheet
- large frying pan
- ladle
- spatula

frying pan

1 Pour the milk into the measuring cup and carefully crack the egg straight into it. Mix the milk and egg together with a fork or small whisk.

2 Sift the flour, baking soda, baking powder, and a pinch of salt into a large mixing bowl. Make a well in the centre of the bowl.

3 Pour the milk and egg mixture into the well in the centre of the flour mixture. Then carefully add the buttermilk and sweet corn.

4 Gently beat the mixture until the ingredients are combined. Cover the mixture with a plate and leave to stand while you cook the bacon.

5 Line a baking sheet with foil and preheat the oven to 177°C (350°F). Put the bacon in the oven and cook for 8-10 minutes on each side, or until crisp.

6 Heat half the oil in the pan and then ladle in the batter to make griddle cakes about 10 cm in diameter. Make sure there is space between the cakes.

7 Cook for 2-3 minutes, until golden underneath. Flip and then cook the other side. Make 12 cakes in this way, adding the rest of the oil when necessary.

Food Facts

Like all dairy foods, milk is an excellent source of calcium and phosphorus, both of which are essential for healthy teeth and bones. Interestingly, there's exactly the same amount of calcium in skim milk as there is in whole milk. Zinc and B vitamins are also provided by milk, along with antibodies, that help boost the immune system and the digestive system.

milk

Mini Pizzas

Traditionally, a pizza base is made using yeast which helps it to rise. These yeast-free mini pizzas mean that the base does not need time-consuming kneading or rising, however, they still taste light and crisp.

Tasty Twists

You can add any of your favourite toppings in step 7 before sprinkling the cheddar. Mushrooms, peppers, onions, pineapple, tuna, shrimp, ham, olives, pepperoni, and cooked chicken all taste great!

Ingredients

whole wheat flour

- 550 mL (2¼ cups) white or whole wheat self-rising flour (plus extra for dusting)
- 2 mL (½ tsp) salt
- 125–150 mL (½–⅔ cup) low fat milk
- 60 mL (4 tbsp) olive oil

mozzarella

Topping:
- 1 quantity Tomato Dipping Sauce (see page 68–69)
- 150g (5 ½ oz) ball mozzarella (drained)
- 125 mL (½ cup) old cheddar (grated)

Equipment

- sieve
- large mixing bowl
- wooden spoon
- rolling pin
- 2 large baking sheets
- spoon

sieve

mixing bowl

rolling pin

1 Preheat the oven to 200°C (400°F). Sift the flour and salt into a mixing bowl, and then make a well in the centre of the mixture.

2 Pour the milk and oil into the well. Mix with a wooden spoon until the flour and liquids start to come together and form a soft dough.

Did you know?
More than 5 billion pizzas are sold worldwide each year. According to a recent poll, children aged between 3 and 11 prefer pizza to all other foods for lunch and dinner.

3 Lightly dust a work top and your hands with flour. Tip the dough out of the bowl and knead it for about 1 minute to form a smooth ball.

4 Dust 2 baking sheets with flour. Divide the dough into 4 smaller balls. Using a rolling pin, roll each piece into a 15 cm circle.

Food Facts
Cheese provides valuable amounts of protein and calcium. However, cheese—especially hard cheese like cheddar—is high in saturated fat so try to eat only moderate amounts. Choose an older cheese, as its strong flavour means that you need less.

cheddar cheese

5 Carefully place 2 dough bases on each baking sheet. Top each base with 1–2 tablespoons of the Tomato Dipping Sauce (see p.68–69).

6 Using the back of a spoon, spread the tomato sauce in an even layer almost to the edge of the pizza base. Slice the mozzarella ball into 8-12 pieces.

7 Add the mozzarella and any other toppings. Top with the cheddar cheese. Bake the pizzas for 10 mins or until the base has risen and the top is golden.

Turkey Burgers

This tasty, low-fat turkey burger is a healthy winner when partnered with a high-fibre bun. It's sure to get gobbled up in no time!

Tasty Twists

Vegetarians could use the Veggie Burgers recipe on p.34, and meat eaters could try ground pork, beef, or lamb as a tasty alternative burger mix.

See p.35 for the Burger Relish recipe.

Ingredients

- 1 small onion
- 1 apple
- 450 g (1 lb) lean ground turkey, chicken, beef, pork, or lamb
- 1 small egg
- flour
- salt and pepper

burger buns

To serve

- seeded burger buns (preferably whole wheat)
- lettuce leaves
- sliced tomatoes
- relish (see p.35)

apples

whole wheat flour

lettuce leaves

Equipment

- grater
- mixing bowl
- wooden spoon
- small bowl
- fork or whisk
- plastic wrap and foil
- large plate
- baking sheet
- tongs

wooden spoon

mixing bowl

1 Peel and then finely chop the onion. Leaving the skin on, coarsely grate the apple. When you can see the core and seeds—it's done!

2 Put the onion and apple into a mixing bowl and add the ground meat. Stir or use your hands to break up the meat and mix it with the onion and apple.

3 Crack an egg into a separate bowl and lightly beat the yolk and white together, using a fork or whisk. This will help bind the burger mixture together.

4 Pour the beaten egg into the meat, onion, and apple mixture. Season, then mix it all together with clean hands—this part is messy but a lot of fun!

5 Lightly cover a plate and your hands with flour. Take a handful of the mixture and shape into a round, flat burger. Put it onto the floured plate.

6 Do the same with the rest of the mixture and then lightly dust all 6 burgers with flour. Cover with plastic wrap and chill for at least 30 minutes.

Food Facts

Turkey is a versatile meat that contains an array of valuable nutrients, including iron, zinc, and selenium. It is a good source of B vitamins, which are essential for the body's processing of foods. Turkey is also high in protein and low in fat, making it one of the healthiest meats of all.

ground turkey

7 Preheat the broiler to medium. Place the burgers on a foil-covered sheet, and cook them for 8 minutes on each side, or until cooked through.

Main Meals

Balance is the key to a healthy main meal, so imagine that your plate is divided into three parts. Vegetables and fruit should form the main part of your meal (about half of your plate); there should also be a protein food such as meat, fish, poultry, eggs, nuts, or beans and, finally, some whole grains and carbohydrates. Eat at least 2 hours before going to bed to give your body time to digest your food properly. There are great recipe ideas in this section, but here are some simple ideas to tempt your tastebuds.

Canada's Food Guide recommends filling half your plate with vegetables and fruit, a quarter with protein foods, and the rest with whole grains. Try to eat a variety of healthy foods every day.

Pasta Salad

Cook 125g (4½oz) pasta according to the package instructions, drain, and then stir in 60 mL (4 tbsp) pesto (see p.64–65). Cut a 150g (5½oz) ball of mozzarella into bite-sized pieces and stir into the pasta. Add a handful of basil leaves, 12 halved cherry tomatoes, and a sprinkling of pine nuts.

Sausage Veggie Roast

Preheat the oven to 200°C (400°F). Place chunks of butternut squash, potato, wedges of onion, and some sausages in a roasting pan, with 15 mL (1 tbsp) olive oil. Roast in the oven for 20 minutes. Remove from the oven, turn the vegetables and sausages so they brown evenly, then add some cherry tomatoes. Return to the oven for another 10–15 minutes.

Steamed Veggies

Steamed vegetables are cooked over water, not in water, as they are when boiled. This preserves many of the vitamins, especially the water-soluble ones.

Couscous

Couscous is a tasty alternative to rice or pasta. Put 325 mL (1⅓ cups) couscous into a bowl and pour in enough boiling water or stock to just cover the couscous. Stir the couscous with a fork and leave to stand for 5–10 minutes, or until the liquid has been absorbed. Fluff up the couscous with a fork before serving.

Baked Beans

For homemade baked beans, combine 150 mL (⅔ cup) pinto beans (drained and rinsed), 150 mL (⅔ cup) stewed tomatoes, 5 mL (1 tsp) Dijon mustard, and 15 mL (1 tbsp) each of olive oil, Worcestershire sauce, maple syrup, and tomato purée in a saucepan. Bring to a boil then reduce the heat. Half-cover the pan and simmer for 15–20 minutes until the sauce has thickened, stirring occasionally.

Nuts and Seeds

Sprinkle a handful of nuts and seeds over salads, stir-fries, noodles, or rice. Just a handful can boost levels of vitamins B and E, iron, zinc, and omega-6 essential fats. Walnuts and pumpkin seeds also contain omega-3 fats.

Stir Fry

Stir-frying is a healthy and quick way of cooking. Cut the ingredients into similar size pieces so they cook equally and use a small amount of oil. Carrots, peppers, snow peas, zucchinis, mushrooms, onions, and beansprouts all taste great stir-fried.

Mashed Potatoes

For tasty and colourful mashed potatoes, try adding carrots, celery, squash, or sweet potato. Use equal amounts of potato and the vegetable of your choice and cook in boiling water for 15–20 minutes, or until tender. Drain, then return to the pan and mash. Add milk and a little butter to make it creamy.

Italian Tuna Pasta

Tuna is a good source of low-fat protein and is a very common addition to pasta in Italy. Although canned tuna is slightly lower in omega-3 fat than fresh, it still provides valuable brain-boosting nutrients. Best if all, this simple dish takes only minutes to make!

Tasty Twists

Serve with a green vegetable. Steamed broccoli is a great choice—the vitamin C in the tomato sauce will help your body absorb the iron in the broccoli. To give the sauce a protein boost, add some canned beans, such as chick peas.

Ingredients

- 625 mL (2½ cups) pasta bows
- 30 mL (2 tbsp) olive oil
- 2 large cloves garlic (crushed)
- 5 mL (1 tsp) dried oregano (optional)
- 10 mL (2 tsp) tomato purée
- 796 mL (28 fl oz) can diced tomatoes
- 2 mL (½ tsp) sugar (optional)
- 170 g (6 oz) canned tuna in olive oil (drained and broken up into chunks)
- salt and pepper

garlic

pasta bows

Equipment

- small sharp knife
- cutting board
- medium saucepan with lid
- large saucepan
- wooden spoon
- colander
- tablespoon

colander

saucepan

1 Bring a large saucepan of water to a boil. Add the pasta and cook according to the packet instructions, until the pasta is tender but not too soft.

2 Meanwhile, heat the oil in a saucepan over a medium heat. Fry the garlic for 1 minute. Stir in the oregano, the diced tomatoes and tomato purée.

3 Bring the sauce to a boil and reduce the heat. Half cover the pan and simmer for 15 mins or until the sauce has reduced by a third and thickened.

You only need to add sugar in step 4 if the tomatoes taste a little sharp.

Food Facts

Tomatoes get their red colour from lycopene. It is one of the few nutrients that is more easily absorbed by the body when it is heated or in a concentrated form, such as in a purée or sauce. Great for strengthening our immune systems and fighting colds, lycopene is an important antioxidant.

tomatoes

4 Stir the tuna into the sauce. Half-cover the pan and heat through for 2 mins, stirring occasionally. Add some sugar to the sauce if necessary and season.

5 Drain the pasta but save 30 mL (2 tbsp) of the water. Return the pasta to the saucepan. Add the water and stir in the sauce until the pasta is coated.

Mixed Bean Burritos

A burrito is a delicious Mexican dish consisting of a rolled up flour tortilla filled with meat or vegetables.

Guacamole is the perfect accompaniment.

Ingredients

- 15 mL (1 tbsp) olive oil
- 1 large onion (chopped)
- 540 mL (19 fl oz) can mixed beans (drained and rinsed)
- 5 mL (1 tsp) dried oregano
- ½ x 796 mL (28 fl oz) can diced tomatoes
- 15 mL (1 tbsp) tomato purée
- 5 mL (1 tsp) ground cumin

onion

- few drops Tabasco (optional)
- salt and pepper

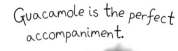
cheddar cheese

To serve

- 4 soft flour tortillas
- 125 mL (½ cup) old cheddar cheese (grated)
- store-bought guacamole (optional)

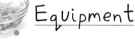
tortillas

Equipment

- small sharp knife
- cutting board
- medium saucepan with lid
- large spoon
- spatula or wooden spoon

cutting board

saucepan

1 Heat the oil in a medium-sized saucepan. Add the onion and cook, stirring occasionally, for 8 minutes until it is softened and slightly golden.

2 Add the oregano, diced tomatoes, tomato purée, and cumin to the saucepan. Tip the beans into the pan, stir and bring to a boil.

3 When bubbling, reduce the heat to low. Half cover with a lid and simmer for 10 minutes. Stir the beans occasionally to stop them sticking.

4 Taste the beans and add salt and pepper along with a few drops of Tabasco if you like. Cook for another 5 minutes, stirring occasionally.

Tasty Twists

Many other toppings can be added to the beans before rolling up the tortilla. Try chopped lettuce, salsa, sour cream, or thin slices of jalapeno peppers!

Food Facts

Beans are also known as legumes. They are an excellent combination of protein and carbohydrates, and what's more they are low in fat. Beans also contain a lot of fibre, which is good for your digestive system.

mixed beans

Did you know?

The word burrito means "little donkey" in Spanish. It is thought that the dish gets its name because a rolled up tortilla resembles the ear of a donkey!

5 Warm the tortilla in a microwave. Place each one on a plate and top with the bean stew. Sprinkle with cheddar and top with a dollop of guacamole.

6 Fold in one end of the tortilla and then carefully fold over one side. Gently roll the tortilla over to make a tight and secure burrito.

Chicken Drumsticks

The yogourt marinade gives the chicken drumsticks a lightly spiced flavour but also keeps them tender and tasty. All you need is a simple green salad and warm naan bread for a delicious meal!

These would also taste great cooked on a barbecue!

lemon

Ingredients

- 4 skinless chicken drumsticks

Marinade
- juice of ½ lemon
- 125 mL (½ cup) thick plain yogourt
- 30 mL (2 tbsp) tandoori spice blend

- 15 mL (1 tbsp) sunflower oil

To serve
- mango chutney (optional)
- 4 small naan bread
- lettuce

lettuce

naan bread

Equipment

- paper towel
- spoon
- large, shallow dish
- bowl
- plastic wrap
- baking sheet
- pastry brush
- tongs
- oven mitts

oven mitts

1 Pat the chicken with a paper towel. Make three deep cuts in each drumstick and place them in a large, shallow dish. Squeeze the lemon juice over the drumsticks.

2 Put the yogourt and tandoori spices in a bowl then mix together. Spoon the yogourt marinade over the chicken until it is completely covered.

3 Cover the drumsticks with plastic wrap and chill them for at least 1 hour to marinate. After 50 minutes, preheat the oven to 200°C (400°F).

4 Brush the oil over the bottom of a baking sheet. Place the chicken drumsticks on the baking sheet and cook them in the oven for 15 minutes.

5 After 15 minutes, turn the chicken over and spoon on any remaining marinade. Cook the drumsticks for a further 15 minutes or until cooked through.

6 Check that the chicken is cooked through. (There should be no trace of pinkness.) Try serving with mango chutney, warm naan bread, and lettuce.

chicken

Pesto Pasta

Pasta is the ultimate quick, simple, and nutritious meal. Try stirring in a spoonful of homemade pesto for an equally quick and mouthwateringly tasty sauce.

Tasty Twists

Add peas, green beans, carrots, or cauliflower along with the broccoli for an extra veggie boost. For extra protein, add some cooked chicken or stir-fried tofu.

You could swirl a spoonful of pesto in soup, stir it into bread dough, or spread it over toast.

spaghetti   salt   pepper

Ingredients

- 250g (9oz) spaghetti
- 15–20 small florets broccoli

pine nuts

Pesto
- 2 large cloves garlic (roughly chopped)
- 45 mL (3 tbsp) pine nuts

garlic

- 60 mL (4 tbsp) fresh finely grated Parmesan cheese (plus extra for serving)
- 1 large bunch fresh basil leaves (60g/2½ oz)
- 75 mL (⅓ cup) olive oil
- salt and pepper

basil leaves

Equipment

- small sharp knife
- cutting board
- food processor
- jar with a lid
- large saucepan
- wooden spoon
- colander
- pasta spoon

colander

cutting board

1 Put the garlic and pine nuts in a food processor and blend until coarsely chopped. Next, add the Parmesan and basil and blend again until a coarse purée.

2 Pour the olive oil into the food processor and blend to make a smooth mixture. Season to taste. Transfer the pesto to a jar with a lid.

Did you know?

Pesto is an Italian sauce from the city of Genoa that dates back to Roman times. The word "pesto" comes from an Italian word meaning "to crush" in Italian.

3 Fill a large saucepan three-quarters full of water. Add 5 mL (1 tsp) of salt and bring the water to a boil. Lower the pasta into the pan.

4 Cook the pasta according to the instructions on the package. About 4 minutes before the pasta is cooked, add the broccoli and simmer.

5 Drain the pasta and broccoli but reserve 30 mL (2 tbsp) of the cooking water. Return the pasta and broccoli to the pan with the cooking water.

Food Facts

Broccoli is a super-veggie, thanks to its impressive range of nutrients, from B vitamins and iron to zinc and potassium. Broccoli belongs to the same family as cabbage, cauliflower, kale, and Brussels sprouts.

broccoli

6 Add enough pesto to coat the pasta and broccoli (you may have some left over). Stir and divide the pasta between four shallow bowls.

Griddled Chicken and Potato Salad

This healthy dish is really easy to make, and bursting with colour and flavour!

Helpful Hints

To check that the chicken is thoroughly cooked, insert a skewer or the tip of a knife into the thickest part—there should be no sign of any pink. If the chicken is not completely done, cook it for another minute or two.

The chicken could also be served with a green salad or on a bed of rice.

Ingredients

- 4 skinless chicken breasts (each about 150g/5½oz)

Marinade
- 10 mL (2 tsp) paprika
- 45 mL (3 tbsp) olive oil

Potato Salad
- 400g (14oz) baby new potatoes (cut in half if necessary)
- 2 green onions (finely chopped)
- 8 cherry tomatoes (halved)
- 45 mL (3 tbsp) chopped fresh mint
- 30 mL (2 tbsp) extra-virgin olive oil
- 15 mL (1 tbsp) lemon juice

green onions

cherry tomatoes

Equipment

- large shallow dish
- tablespoon ● plastic wrap
- griddle (or frying pan)
- tongs
- small sharp knife
- cutting board
- medium saucepan
- salad bowl

tongs

sharp knife

1 Mix the paprika and the olive oil in a large, shallow dish. Add the chicken and spoon over the marinade. Cover with plastic wrap and chill for 30 minutes.

Food Facts

A griddle is similar to a frying pan but it is usually square and has a ridged base. It is sometimes called a grill pan. This design makes griddling a healthier way of cooking because most of the fat collects in the ridges of the pan, rather than in the food itself. Meat, fish, and vegetables can all be cooked on a griddle. As well as being a healthy way to cook, griddling gives food a delicious, slightly barbecued flavour.

griddle

2 Heat a griddle pan until it is very hot. Reduce the heat to medium and place 2 chicken breasts in the pan. Griddle for 6 minutes on one side.

3 Carefully turn the chicken over using tongs. Spoon over a little of the marinade and then cook for another 6 minutes, or until cooked through.

4 Cook the remaining chicken breasts in the same way, making sure there is no trace of pink in the middle. Serve with the potato salad.

1 Put the potatoes in a medium saucepan and cover with water. Bring to a boil and cook the potatoes for 10 minutes or until they are tender.

2 Drain the potatoes and leave them to cool in a bowl. Finely chop the green onions and halve the tomatoes. Put them in the bowl. Add the mint.

3 Mix the extra-virgin olive oil and lemon juice together, using a fork. Then pour the dressing over the salad and stir well to mix it in.

Lamb Kebabs and Tomato Dip

Soak the wooden skewers in water for 30 minutes to prevent them burning.

These kebabs contain just the right amount of spice to give them plenty of flavour without being too hot and spicy.

Did you know?
Many people believe that eating garlic prevents ageing. (It also keeps vampires away, of course!)

lean minced lamb

Ingredients

- 450 g (1 lb) lean ground lamb
- 1 small onion (finely chopped or processed)
- 2 cloves garlic (crushed)
- 2 mL (½ tsp) ground cinnamon
- 10 mL (2 tsp) ground cumin
- 5 mL (1 tsp) ground coriander
- olive oil (for brushing)
- salt and pepper

Tomato Dipping Sauce
- 30 mL (2 tbsp) olive oil
- 2 cloves garlic (crushed)
- 325 mL (1⅓ cups) drained canned tomatoes
- 15 mL (1 tbsp) sun-dried tomato purée (or tomato purée)
- 2 mL (½ tsp) sugar

olive oil

Equipment

- medium saucepan
- large mixing bowl
- wooden spoon
- baking sheet
- 12 wooden or metal skewers
- tongs

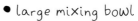

tongs

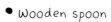

wooden skewer

wooden spoon

1 Pour the olive oil into a pan and heat gently. Fry the garlic for 1 minute, stirring constantly. Add the tomatoes, tomato purée and sugar and bring to a boil.

2 Reduce the heat, partially cover the pan and simmer for 15 minutes. Stir the sauce occasionally to prevent it sticking to the bottom of the pan.

Tasty Twists

For an Italian flavour, replace the cinnamon, cumin and coriander with 10 mL (2 tsp) dried oregano and 30 mL (2 tbsp) chopped sun-dried tomatoes. For an Indian flavour, try 15 mL (1 tbsp) mild curry powder.

1 Put the ground lamb in a mixing bowl and break it up using a fork. Add the chopped onion, garlic, cinnamon, cumin, and coriander to the bowl.

2 Season with salt and pepper and then stir the ingredients until they are all combined. Preheat the oven to 220°C (425°F) and lightly oil a baking sheet.

3 Divide the lamb mixture into 12 pieces. Shape each one into a sausage and then thread them onto the skewers. Press or roll to lengthen the kebabs.

4 Place the lamb kebabs onto the baking sheet. Bake them for 15–20 minutes, turning them over halfway, until golden all over and cooked through.

Food Facts

Every country in the world includes onions in its cooking. Along with garlic, onion has become an essential flavouring in a wide variety of dishes. For centuries, onions and garlic have also been used in all kinds of traditional remedies. Both are antibacterial and antiviral, helping to fight colds and relieve asthma and hayfever.

garlic

onion

Salmon Parcels

Salmon is full of brain-boosting, healthy oils that help with concentration and memory. If you are not usually a fan of fish, this tasty recipe might just win you over!

Did you know?

Japan consumes the highest amount of salmon per person, and has the lowest level of heart disease in the world.

Vegetarians could use a selection of vegetables, such as carrot, red pepper, snow peas, broccoli, green onions, or zucchinis.

Ingredients

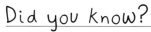
carrot

- 30 mL (2 tbsp) sesame seeds
- 4 slices fresh ginger (peeled and cut into thin strips)
- 30 mL (2 tbsp) soy sauce
- 60 mL (4 tbsp) orange juice
- 4 thick salmon fillets (about 150 g/5½ oz each)
- 1 carrot (cut into thin strips)
- 1 red pepper (de-seeded and cut into thin strips)
- 3 green onions (cut into thin strips)
- salt and black pepper
- 250 g (9 oz) noodles

fresh ginger

noodles

Equipment

sharp knife

- small sharp knife
- cutting board
- frying pan
- baking sheet
- baking parchment

cutting board

1 Preheat the oven to 200°C (400°F). Toast the sesame seeds in a dry frying pan until golden. Remove from the pan and set aside.

2 Cut the baking parchment into 4 pieces, at least twice the size of the salmon fillets. Place each piece of salmon on a piece of baking parchment.

3 Arrange a mixture of the carrot, red pepper, green onion, and ginger strips on top of each salmon fillet. Drizzle over the soy sauce and orange juice.

4 Season with salt and pepper. Carefully fold in the top and bottom of each parcel and then gather up the sides. Gently fold to make 4 loose parcels.

5 Put the parcels on a baking sheet and bake for 15 minutes. Add the noodles to a pan of boiling water and cook, following the instructions on the package.

Tasty Twists

Chicken breasts would also taste delicious cooked in this way. Follow the recipe but bake the chicken slightly longer than the salmon —about 20-25 minutes, or until cooked through.

6 Remove the fish from the oven and leave to cool slightly before opening the parcels. Serve with the noodles and a sprinkling of sesame seeds.

Food Facts

Salmon is an excellent source of polyunsaturated fatty acids, known as omega-3. These are the healthier kind of fats and have been shown to help reduce heart disease. They are good for the brain, skin, eyes, and nerves, too. (See p.14–15).

salmon

Roasted Vegetable Pasta

Roasting vegetables is a great way to make them sweet and melt-in-your mouth tasty, without losing their nutrients.

Tasty Twists

Butternut squash, eggplant, leeks, or carrots would also taste great. Meat lovers could add ham or canned tuna in step 2, or chicken, bacon, or sausage that has been browned first.

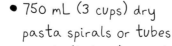

Ingredients

- 1 eggplant
- 1 large zucchini
- 1 large red onion
- 6 cloves garlic (whole)
- 1 large red pepper (de-seeded)
- 45 mL (3 tbsp) olive oil
- 12 cherry tomatoes
- 750 mL (3 cups) dry pasta spirals or tubes
- 60 mL (4 tbsp) low-fat sour cream or crème fraiche
- 150 mL (⅔ cup) old cheddar cheese (grated)
- 15 mL (1 tbsp) wholegrain mustard
- salt and pepper

eggplant

cheddar cheese

Equipment

- small sharp knife
- cutting board
- roasting pan
- large saucepan
- wooden spoon
- small mixing bowl
- teaspoon

saucepan

mixing bowl

1 Preheat the oven to 200°C (400°F). Slice the eggplant, zucchini, and red pepper into bite-sized chunks. Cut the onion into 8 wedges.

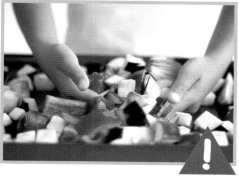

2 Put the eggplant, zucchini, onion, garlic, and red pepper in a roasting pan. Drizzle the oil over the vegetables and turn them so they are coated in oil.

Food Facts

Red, green, and yellow peppers are bursting with vitamin C and are great for healthy skin, teeth, and bones. Red peppers have an extra benefit —they contain higher amounts of beta-carotene, which is good for fighting viruses.

red peppers

3 Roast for 15 minutes and then remove the pan from the oven. Add the tomatoes and coat them in the oil. Roast for 10 mins or until the vegetables are tender.

4 Meanwhile, bring a large saucepan of water to a boil. Add the pasta and cook according to the package until it is tender but not too soft.

Helpful Hint

There are lots of different pasta shapes to choose from. Opt for one that can "hold" the sauce like penne, rigatoni, or farfalle, rather than long pasta such as spaghetti or tagliatelle.

5 Remove the garlic cloves from the roasting pan. Drain the pasta and add it to the vegetables in the pan. Now peel and finely chop the garlic.

6 Mix the garlic with the sour cream and mustard. Add the sour cream mixture to the pasta and vegetables and sprinkle with the cheddar.

7 Season and stir to mix it all together. Put the pan back in the oven for 5 minutes or until the cheese has melted and everything is warmed through.

Sticky Ribs with Baked Potato

Give pork spare ribs a delicious sticky sweetness with this simple barbeque sauce—they're best eaten with your fingers!

The ribs can be marinated overnight for maximum flavour.

Ingredients

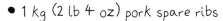

pork spare ribs

- 1 kg (2 lb 4 oz) pork spare ribs
- 4 medium baking potatoes (scrubbed)
- 60 mL (4 tbsp) sour cream (optional)
- 30 mL (2 tbsp) chopped chives (optional)

Marinade

Tabasco

- 30 mL (2 tbsp) honey
- 15 mL (1 tbsp) balsamic vinegar
- 60 mL (4 tbsp) ketchup
- 30 mL (2 tbsp) brown sugar
- 15 mL (1 tbsp) Dijon mustard
- 15 mL (1 tbsp) olive oil
- 3 drops Tabasco (optional)

Equipment

baking sheet

- measuring cup
- fork
- extra-wide foil
- baking sheet
- knife
- oven mitts

extra-wide foil

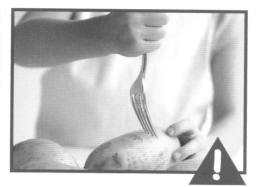

1 Put the marinade ingredients in a measuring cup and mix together. Place the ribs on a large piece of double-thickness foil. Pour the marinade over the ribs.

2 Make sure that the ribs are well coated. Scrunch the foil loosely around the ribs and twist to seal. Leave to marinate in the fridge for at least 1 hour.

3 Preheat the oven to 200°C (400°F). Scrub the potatoes and prick them all over with a fork. Bake the potatoes for 1 hour or until soft in the centre.

4 Remove the foil parcel with the ribs from the fridge and carefully place it onto a baking sheet. Cook them in the oven with the potatoes for 30 minutes.

5 Carefully open up the foil parcel. Cook the ribs in the open parcel for a further 30 minutes, or until they are completely cooked.

Tasty Twists

This delicious marinade could be used to coat chicken, turkey, fish, vegetables, or tofu. You could also try barbecuing instead of roasting.

6 Cut the potatoes in half and open them up. (Take care—they will be hot!) Top each potato with some sour cream and chives. Serve with the ribs.

Food Facts

Baking is a great way to cook potatoes. Not only is it a very simple method of cooking, but there is no need to add any fat. Potatoes are a popular starchy carbohydrate food and provide your body with energy as well as immunity-boosting vitamins B and C, plus iron and potassium. The skin contains the highest concentration of fibre, which helps your digestive system work efficiently.

potatoes

Jambalaya

This is a colourful Creole or Cajun rice dish from Louisiana. It is easy to make because all the ingredients are cooked in the same pot. The recipe can be adapted for vegetarians by swapping the chicken and ham for extra vegetables, meat-free sausages, or tofu.

Tasty Twists

Shrimp, pork, beans, or vegetables, such as peas and zucchinis, would also be tasty in this rice dish.

Ingredients

- 30 mL (2 tbsp) olive oil
- 3 skinless chicken breasts
- 1 large onion (chopped)
- 200 g (7 oz) smoked ham
- 2 large cloves garlic (chopped)
- 1 red pepper (de-seeded and cut into bite-sized pieces)
- 5 mL (1 tsp) paprika
- 1 green chili, de-seeded and finely chopped (optional)
- 5 mL (1 tsp) dried thyme
- 750 mL (3 cups) warm chicken or vegetable stock
- 45 mL (3 tbsp) canned diced tomatoes
- 325 mL (1⅓ cups) brown rice
- 75 mL (⅓ cup) peas
- salt and pepper

pepper

peas

Equipment

- sieve
- small sharp knife
- cutting board
- large saucepan with lid
- wooden spoon
- measuring cup

cutting board

saucepan

1 Put the rice in a sieve and rinse it under cold water until the water runs clear. Washing the rice before cooking stops the grains from sticking together.

2 Chop the onion into small pieces and set aside. Then carefully cut the chicken and ham into bite-sized pieces. Heat the oil in the large saucepan.

3 Fry the chicken and onion for 8 mins over a medium heat until the chicken is golden all over. Stir frequently to prevent the chicken sticking to the pan.

Add the peas 2 minutes before the rice is cooked in step 5 for extra colour and goodness!

Did you know?

One seed of rice yields more than 3,000 grains. Rice is the highest-yielding cereal grain and can grow in many kinds of environments.

Food Facts

Rice is a staple food all over the world, and its cultivation dates back to 5,000 BCE. It is an excellent source of energy. Brown rice is healthier than white rice because it contains fibre and richer amounts of vitamins and minerals. White rice has had the husk, bran, and germ removed, which significantly reduces its nutritional value.

rice

4 Add the ham, garlic, red pepper, and chili, and cook for 2 mins. Add the paprika, thyme, rice, stock, and tomatoes. Stir and bring to a boil.

5 Reduce the heat to low, cover the pan and simmer for 35 mins or until the rice is cooked and the stock is absorbed. Season the rice and stir before serving.

Colourful Kebabs

These are great fun to make and, of course, to eat! They would make a perfect vegetarian dish for a summer barbecue.

Tasty Twists

Cubes of chicken, beef, pork, lamb, or fish like salmon or tuna would all work in this recipe. Mushrooms, eggplant, and green onions could also be added to the red pepper, red onions, and zucchinis.

Soak the wooden skewers in water for 30 minutes to prevent them from burning.

Ingredients

- 250g (9oz) firm tofu
- 2 small zucchinis (each cut into 8 pieces)
- 2 medium red onions (peeled and each cut into 8 wedges)
- 1 medium red pepper (de-seeded and cut into 16 chunks)
- 1.5 L (6½ cups) dry egg noodles
- 15 mL (1 tbsp) toasted sesame seeds (optional)

noodles

Marinade

- 30 mL (2 tbsp) olive oil
- 15 mL (1 tbsp) soy sauce
- 45 mL (3 tbsp) black bean sauce
- 15 mL (1 tbsp) clear honey
- 2 cloves garlic (crushed)
- salt and pepper

red onion

red pepper

Equipment

tongs

- large shallow dish
- large dish ● paper towel
- sharp knife ● baking sheet
- cutting board
- spoon
- 8 wooden or metal skewers
- pastry brush
- saucepan
- tongs and colander

colander

1 Pat the tofu dry with a paper towel and then cut it into 16 cubes. Put the cubes into the dish with the zucchinis, onions, and red pepper.

Tasty Twists

Swap the oriental marinade for a Mediterranean one. Mix together 60 mL (4 tbsp) olive oil, 30 mL (2 tbsp) balsamic vinegar, 2 crushed cloves garlic, and 15 mL (1 tbsp) clear honey.

Food Facts

Tofu is one of the few plant foods that is a complete protein. This means it contains a healthy balance of the amino acids that are essential for repairing and maintaining your body. It is also low in fat and a good source of iron, calcium, magnesium, and vitamins B1, B2, and B3. Firm tofu can be fried, stir-fried, deep-fried, sautéed, or grilled. Because tofu itself is fairly bland, it is best marinated or used in recipes with strongly flavoured ingredients.

tofu

2 Mix the ingredients for the marinade in a large dish. Use a spoon to coat the tofu and vegetables in the marinade. Put in the fridge for at least 1 hour.

3 Preheat the broiler. Thread pieces of red pepper, tofu, red onion, and zucchini onto a skewer. Repeat and then make 7 more kebabs.

4 Place the kebabs on a baking sheet and brush them with the marinade. Broil for 10–12 minutes, turning halfway through and brushing with more marinade.

5 While the kebabs are cooking, bring a pan of water to a boil, add the noodles and cook as instructed on the package. Drain the noodles in a colander.

6 Serve two kebabs per person. Arrange some noodles on a plate and place the kebabs on top. Sprinkle the sesame seeds over the noodles.

Sausage Hotpot

Fruit gives this savoury casserole a natural sweetness and an extra vitamin boost. Enjoy this winter warmer with fluffy mashed potatoes and steamed green vegetables.

Tasty Twists

Turkey, pork, beef, or vegetarian sausages would all work in this recipe. The sausages are browned in step 2 and then slowly cooked through in the oven.

See p.57 for a yummy Mashed Potato recipe idea.

Ingredients

- 2 apples
- 30 mL (2 tbsp) olive oil
- 6-8 sausages (turkey, pork, beef, or vegetarian)
- 1 onion (chopped)
- 1 carrot (diced)
- 2 cloves garlic (finely chopped)
- 5 mL (1 tsp) mixed herbs
- 5 medium slices lean bacon, cut into bite-sized pieces (optional)
- 540 mL (19 fl oz) canned pinto beans (drained and rinsed)
- 395 mL (1⅓ cups) chicken or vegetable stock
- 60 mL (4 tbsp) canned diced tomatoes
- 15 mL (1 tbsp) tomato purée
- salt and pepper

stock

sausages

Equipment

cutting board

- vegetable peeler
- small sharp knife
- cutting board ● tongs
- large ovenproof pan with lid (or large saucepan and large casserole dish with lid)
- wooden spoon
- measuring cup
- oven mitts

saucepan

1 Carefully remove the skin of the apples using a vegetable peeler. Quarter them and remove the cores. Cut the apples into bite-sized pieces.

2 Preheat the oven to 200°C (400°F). Heat the oil in a large saucepan or ovenproof pan and cook the sausages for 5 minutes, or until browned all over.

Food Facts

There could be something in the saying that "an apple a day keeps the doctor away!" Apples are an excellent source of energy and antioxidants, (especially vitamin C), and they help to clear toxins from the body, too.

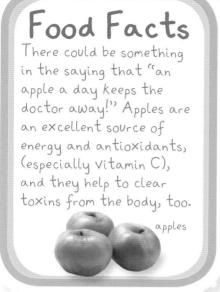

apples

3 Remove the sausages from the pan and set aside. Put the onion and carrot into the pan and fry over a medium heat for 5 minutes, stirring frequently.

4 Next, add the garlic, bacon, and herbs, stir well, and cook for 6 minutes. (Transfer to a large casserole dish if you aren't using an ovenproof pan.)

Did you know?

British people called sausages "bangers" during the Second World War because they contained so much water they exploded when fried!

5 Add the beans, tomatoes, tomato purée, apples, and sausages and stir. Pour in the stock and bring to a boil. Add the beans and stir well.

6 Cover with a lid and place in the preheated oven. Cook for 25 minutes. The sauce should reduce and thicken and the apples will become tender.

7 Take care when removing the casserole dish from the oven as it will be very hot. Season with salt and pepper. Serve with mashed potatoes and vegetables.

Fish Sticks and Sweet Potato Wedges

Try this healthier version of traditional fish fingers and chips —it is easy to make and absolutely delicious!

Did you know?

Fish and chips shops first made an appearance in the UK at the end of the 19th century. Fish and chips quickly became Britain's most popular and famous fast food, and has remained so ever since.

Ingredients

- 400 g (14 oz) cod fillets or other firm white fish (patted dry)
- 175 mL (¾ cup) fine cornmeal or polenta
- 10 mL (2 tsp) Cajun spice mix or paprika (optional)
- 1 egg (beaten)
- salt and pepper
- 30 mL (2 tbsp) olive oil

Sweet Potato Chips
- 2 large sweet potatoes (scrubbed)

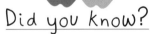
polenta

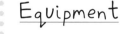
fish fillets

Equipment

- small sharp knife
- cutting board
- paper towel
- roasting pan
- plate
- baking sheet
- tongs

cutting board

baking sheet

1 Preheat the oven to 200°C (400°F). Cut the sweet potatoes in half and then cut each half into smaller wedges. Pat the wedges dry with a paper towel.

2 Put half of the oil into a roasting pan and add the potato wedges. Coat them in the oil and bake for 30 minutes, turning halfway through cooking.

Tasty Twist

You could also use regular baking potatoes instead of the sweet potatoes to make these crisp potato wedges. Just follow the recipe in exactly the same way.

3 Meanwhile, cut the cod into 1 cm strips. Mix the cornmeal or polenta and the spices together on a plate. Season with salt and pepper.

4 One at a time, dip each fish strip into the beaten egg and then roll it in the cornmeal mixture until evenly coated. Repeat with all the fish sticks.

5 Add the remaining oil onto a baking sheet and then the fish sticks. When the wedges have been cooking for 22 minutes, put the fish sticks in the oven.

6 Bake the fish sticks for 8 minutes, turning halfway through. They should be golden and cooked through. Serve with the sweet potato wedges and peas.

Food Facts

Choose orange-fleshed sweet potatoes as they contain higher amounts of beta-carotene than the white variety. Beta-carotene is converted into vitamin A in your body.

sweet potatoes

Rainbow Beef

Stir-frying is a quick and easy way to make a colourful and nutritious meal. You could also serve this stir-fry with rice instead of noodles.

Did you know?
Mangetout means "eat everything" in French. Snow peas are so-called in Europe because you eat the whole vegetable, including the pod.

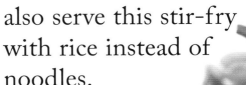

baby corn

Ingredients

- 300 g (⅔ lb) lean beef (cut into thin strips)
- 15 mL (1 tbsp) sunflower oil
- 1.5 L (6½ cups) dry medium egg noodles
- 1 red pepper (de-seeded and cut into thin strips)
- 6 baby corn (halved)
- 250 mL (1 cup) snow peas

snow peas

- 3 green onions (sliced)
- 2 cloves garlic (chopped)
- 10 mL (2 tsp) grated fresh ginger
- 60 mL (4 tbsp) orange juice

Marinade
- 90 mL (6 tbsp) hoisin sauce
- 30 mL (2 tbsp) soy sauce
- 15 mL (1 tbsp) clear honey
- 5 mL (1 tsp) sesame oil

noodles

Equipment

tongs

- small sharp knife
- cutting board
- spoon
- shallow dish
- wok or large frying pan
- spatula or wooden spoon
- tongs
- medium saucepan
- colander

colander

1 Put the marinade ingredients in a shallow dish. Mix them together and then add the beef strips. Coat them in the marinade, cover and set aside for 1 hour.

2 Heat the sunflower oil in a wok or frying pan. Remove the beef strips from the marinade using tongs and carefully put them into the wok or frying pan.

Food Facts

Stir-frying is a healthy method of preparing food because the ingredients are cooked quickly in a minimum amount of oil. This keeps the fat levels down and retains vital vitamins and minerals, which are often destroyed by longer cooking times.

wok

3 Stirring continuously, fry the beef strips on a high heat for 1½ minutes or until browned all over. Remove the beef using the tongs and set aside.

4 Bring a saucepan of water to a boil. Add the noodles to the water, stir to separate them and then cook according to the package instructions until tender.

Tasty Twists

Strips of pork and chicken are a good alternative to the beef, or you could try shrimp or tofu. For the best flavour, it's important to marinate the meat first.

5 Add a little more oil to the wok if it looks dry. Add the red pepper, baby corn, snow peas, and green onions. Stir-fry for 2 minutes.

6 Add the garlic, ginger, beef, and the leftover marinade and stir-fry for 1 minute. Pour in the orange juice and cook, stirring, for another minute.

7 Drain the noodles in a colander and divide them between 4 shallow bowls. Spoon the vegetable and beef stir-fry over the noodles and serve.

Desserts

Being healthy doesn't mean you can't eat dessert—a balanced diet means that you can eat most things, but in moderation. In fact, dessert is an ideal opportunity to get more fruit into your diet! Just remember desserts and cakes can be high in fat, so eat sensibly. There's something for everyone in this section, from fruity gelatin to crunchy cobbler, and from delicious popsicles to apple muffins. Here are some more simple ideas for tasty desserts to try.

Fruit Purée

Simple fruit sauces are a tasty and nutritious accompaniment to yogourt, ice cream, and many other dishes. Use fruit with a soft, juicy texture such as mangoes, berries, or nectarines. Purée your fruit in a blender, adding a little sugar if necessary.

Banana Custard

Mix together equal quantities of plain yogourt and ready-made custard. Pile sliced bananas into a dish and pour over the yogourt mixture. Stewed apples (see p.17) could be used instead.

Fruit Yogourt

Store-bought yogourts are often high in sugar and low in fruit, so make your own healthy versions by stirring fresh fruit purée (see above) into thick plain yogourt.

Mini Crumbles

Preheat the oven to 180°C (350°F). Sprinkle 30 mL (2 tbsp) of the crumble mixture from p.102–103 over 3 peaches or nectarines (halved and pitted). Place the fruit on a baking dish, and pour a little water into the dish to prevent the fruit from drying out. Bake for 20 minutes.

Chocolate Banana

Preheat the oven to 180°C (350°F). Slice a banana lengthwise, but not all the way through. Press chocolate chips into the gap and then wrap the banana in a foil. Bake for 20 minutes, until the chocolate has melted.

Homemade Fruit Spread

Put 150 mL (⅔ cup) dried apricots and 150 mL (⅔ cup) dried dates in a saucepan with 500 mL (2 cups) water. Bring to a boil, reduce the heat, cover, and simmer for 45 minutes. Transfer to a blender, add 75 mL (5 tbsp) of water and blend to a purée. Store in a jar in the fridge for up to 1 week.

Popcorn

Pour 15 mL (1 tbsp) sunflower oil into a medium saucepan. Heat the oil then add a thin layer of popcorn (one kernel deep). Put the lid on the pan and cook over a medium heat, shaking the pan occasionally, until the corn has popped. Caution—don't remove the lid until the sound of popping has stopped!

Warm Fruit Salad

Cook your favourite dried fruits in a little water over a low heat for about 20 minutes, or until soft and plump. Add a cinnamon stick and a little ground nutmeg if you like and serve with plain yogourt.

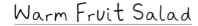

Banana Ice Cream

Wrap a peeled banana in plastic wrap. Freeze for 2 hours or until solid then remove the plastic wrap and whiz in a food processor until roughly chopped. Serve in a bowl with a drizzle of maple syrup and a sprinkling of nuts.

Melon Fruit Bowl

This colourful dessert is packed with the tasty goodness of fresh fruit. Best of all, you can eat the "bowl" afterwards!

Did you know?
There is more sugar in a lemon than in a strawberry! (And strawberries are the only fruit whose seeds grow on the outside.)

Ingredients

- ½ large cantaloupe melon
- 250–375 mL (1–1½ cups) fruit such as apricots, grapes (halved), plums, strawberries, raspberries, blackberries, slices of nectarine, peach, orange, apple, or kiwi
- 60 mL (4 tbsp) orange juice

strawberries

orange juice

Equipment

- sharp knife
- cutting board
- melon baller or spoon
- large mixing bowl

melon baller

1 Scoop the seeds out of the centre of the melon and throw them away. Slice a sliver off the base of the melon so it stands up and place it on a serving plate.

Food Facts

Melons, especially those with orange flesh, contain plentiful amounts of beta-carotene. This is necessary for good vision, healthy skin, and growth. Vitamin C is also found in juicy melons.

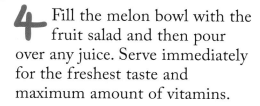

melon

2 Use a melon baller or spoon to scoop out most of the melon flesh. Leave an even 1 cm border in your hollowed out bowl shape.

3 Prepare the rest of the fruit by washing, peeling, slicing, and de-seeding as appropriate. Mix with the orange juice and melon balls in a large bowl.

4 Fill the melon bowl with the fruit salad and then pour over any juice. Serve immediately for the freshest taste and maximum amount of vitamins.

Tropical Yogourt Ice

Bursting with vitamins from the fresh fruit, this cool and creamy yogourt ice is a healthy alternative to ice cream. Plain yogourt has a smooth, creamy taste but is much lower in fat than cream. It contains beneficial bacteria that are good for your digestive system and is also rich in calcium.

Tasty Twists

Strawberries, plums, nectarines, raspberries, and peaches taste just as good as the mango and banana. You will need about 450 g (1 lb) fruit.

Did you know?

More than 50% of the world's mangoes are grown in India. Mangoes belong to the same family as the cashew, pistachio, and poison ivy!

Ingredients

- 2 medium ripe mangoes
- 2 medium bananas (peeled)
- 500 mL (2 cups) thick plain yogourt
- 45 mL (3 tbsp) icing sugar
- squeeze of lemon juice

yogourt

bananas

Equipment

- sharp knife
- cutting board
- blender or food processor
- spoon
- plastic container with lid
- whisk or fork
- ice cream scoop

ice cream scoop

1 To prepare each mango, cut away the two sides close to the stone. Taking the two large slices, cut the flesh into a criss-cross pattern down to the skin.

2 Press each mango half inside out and carefully cut off the cubes of mango. Cut away any remaining mango near the pit. Repeat with the second mango.

3 Break or slice the bananas into chunks and put them into a blender. Then add the mango, yogourt, sugar, and a squeeze of lemon juice.

Remove the ice cream from the fridge 30 mins before you want to eat it.

4 Blend until the mixture becomes thick and creamy. Pour the mixture into a shallow container, securely attach the lid, and put it into the freezer.

5 After 2–3 hours, whisk the mixture with a fork to break down any ice crystals. Freeze and repeat after 3 hours to give the yogourt ice a creamy texture.

Food Facts

Mangoes are rich in vitamin C and beta-carotene, and are a good source of vitamins A and B. However, these nutrients are greatly reduced when the mangoes are cooked.

mangoes

Peachy Orange Popsicles

These refreshing popsicles only take a few minutes to make and are a fun way to ensure that you eat fruit! Add thick plain yogourt to make a frozen yogourt popsicle.

Did you know?

Peaches are native to Northwest China. In Canada, peaches are grown mostly in British Columbia and Ontario.

Ingredients

- 3 ripe peaches or nectarines
- 300 mL (1¼ cups) orange juice
- 15–30 mL (1–2 tbsp) icing sugar or to taste
- 4 heaped spoonfuls canned fruit salad in natural juice, drained (optional)

glacé cherries

orange juice

Equipment

- small sharp knife ● tablespoon
- cutting board
- large slotted spoon
- 2 bowls
- blender
- 4 popsicle moulds

popsicle moulds

1 Peaches can be tricky and messy to peel, so here is a simple way to do it. Using a slotted spoon, lower the fruit into a bowl of boiling water.

2 After about 30 seconds, remove the fruit and then immediately plunge it into a bowl of cold water. The skin should peel away easily.

Tasty Twists

You could layer different fruits such as berries, mangoes, kiwis, oranges, or bananas but you must partially freeze each layer for 45 minutes before adding the next or they will all mix together.

3 Carefully slice the fruit away from the pit and put it into a blender. Add the orange juice and 15 mL (1 tbsp) of the icing sugar.

4 Blend the peaches, orange juice, and icing sugar until smooth and frothy. Taste the juice and add the rest of the icing sugar if necessary.

Food Facts

Peaches are full of vitamin C and are also a good source of potassium and fibre. They contain beta-carotene, which the body converts to vitamin A. Nectarines are a smooth-skinned variety of peaches.

peaches

5 Spoon half of the fruit salad into the 4 moulds. Pour the juice over each mould until it is half full. Add the rest of the fruit salad and top up with fruit juice.

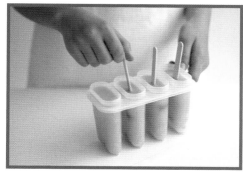

6 Insert the stick into the mould then freeze for at least 6 hours. Before eating, take the popsicles out of the freezer and let them soften slightly.

Sunshine Gelatin

Even though this healthier version of gelatin is made with fruit juice and fresh oranges, it still contains sugar and should only be eaten as an occasional treat.

Tasty Twists

Mango, nectarine, peach, or cherry would all taste great in this recipe, but any fruity flavours of gelatin would work well.

Did you know?

Gelatin was first eaten in Ancient Egypt. In the UK, jelly moulds and ice cream are a popular dessert, especially for children.

Ingredients

- 2 oranges
- 85 g (3 oz) package lemon gelatin granules
- 175 mL (¾ cup) fresh orange juice

oranges

Equipment

- small sharp knife
- plate or cutting board
- 600 mL (2½ cups) gelatin mould or glass bowl
- measuring cup
- serving plate

sharp knife

mixing bowl

1 Cut a thin slice off one end of an orange to help it stand up on a plate or cutting board. Carefully slice downwards to remove the skin and pith.

2 Cut the orange into thin, round slices. Arrange some of the orange slices on the base and sides of the gelatin mould or glass bowl.

3 Pour the orange juice into a measuring cup, add the gelatin granules and carefully top up with boiling water to make 600 mL (2½ cups) in total.

Helpful Hint

Pineapple, kiwi, papaya, and figs are not suitable for this recipe because they contain enzymes which break down the gelatin and stop it from setting.

4 Stir gently until the gelatin granules dissolve. Carefully pour half of the warm liquid gelatin into the gelatin mould, on top of the orange slices.

5 Put the remaining orange slices on top of the gelatin and then pour over the rest of the liquid mixture. Leave to cool, then chill for at least 6 hours to set.

6 Place a serving plate on top of the mould and then carefully turn it over so the plate is underneath—the gelatin should slip out easily onto the plate.

Food Facts

Like all citrus fruits, oranges are a great source of vitamin C and they are full of natural sweetness and taste. It's better to use freshly squeezed fruit juice rather than juice made from concentrates, because a lot of the nutrients are lost during the manufacturing process.

orange juice

95

Fruit Sticks with Chocolate Orange Dip

This dessert is fun to make, and even more fun to eat! It's great for parties and works with any of your favourite fruits.

chocolate

Ingredients

- ½ cantaloupe melon (seeds scooped out)
- 1 small pineapple
- 3 kiwi fruits (peeled)
- 18 strawberries

Chocolate Orange Dip

- 175 mL (¾ cup) milk
- 100 g (3½ oz) milk or dark chocolate (broken into tiny pieces)
- zest of 1 orange (grated)

Equipment

- medium saucepan
- wooden spoon
- sharp knife
- cutting board
- melon baller or spoon
- 18 wooden skewers

strawberries

melon

melon baller

1 Pour the milk into a saucepan and add the grated orange zest. Bring the milk to a boil. Carefully remove the pan from the heat, and add the chocolate.

2 Gently stir the milk until the chocolate has melted. Pour the sauce into a bowl and leave it to cool slightly while you prepare the fruit sticks.

Tasty Twists

Use any of your favourite fruits in this recipe. The Fruit Sticks taste equally delicious dipped into a yogourt or fruit sauce (see p.86-87).

1 Top and tail the pineapple using a knife. Hold the pineapple upright on a cutting board and cut downwards to remove the skin.

2 Slice the pineapple and quarter each slice. Cut off the core and eyes. Halve the melon and scoop out the flesh in balls, with a melon baller or spoon.

3 Top and tail each kiwi fruit and holding the fruit upright, slice downward away from you to remove the skin, then cut it into large chunks.

4 Thread some pineapple, a melon ball, a strawberry, and a chunk of kiwi onto a skewer. Repeat for all 18 sticks and serve with the chocolate dip.

Food Facts

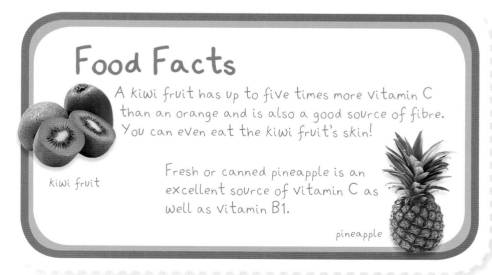

A kiwi fruit has up to five times more vitamin C than an orange and is also a good source of fibre. You can even eat the kiwi fruit's skin!

kiwi fruit

Fresh or canned pineapple is an excellent source of vitamin C as well as vitamin B1.

pineapple

Fruit Sundae

This fruity ice cream sundae is a refreshing, vitamin-filled treat. Any of your favourite fruits will taste great in this recipe. If you don't have time to make the Tropical Yogourt Ice, you can use two extra scoops of vanilla ice cream instead.

Helpful Hints

Try to buy strawberries in season for the best, most nutritious fruit. The lemon juice enhances the flavour of the strawberries and also prevents the sauce oxidizing or discolouring.

Ingredients

- 8 small scoops Tropical Yogourt Ice (see p.90-91 for recipe)
- 4 small scoops Vanilla ice cream
- a selection of fresh fruits, such as strawberries, mango, kiwi fruits, or raspberries (the amount depends on size of your glasses)
- toasted flaked almonds (optional)

Strawberry Sauce

- 650 mL (2⅔ cups) strawberries
- squeeze of fresh lemon juice
- a little icing sugar

mango

raspberries

Equipment

kiwi

- sharp knife
- cutting board
- sieve
- blender or food processor
- ice cream scoop
- 4 sundae glasses

banana

1 Cut the stems off the strawberries, slice them in half, and then purée them in a blender or food processor until they are smooth with no lumps.

2 Press the strawberry purée through a sieve, using the back of a spoon, to remove the seeds. Stir in a little lemon juice and icing sugar to sweeten.

3 Put a scoop of Tropical Yogourt Ice into the glass and add a spoonful of Strawberry Sauce. Add some fruit and a scoop of vanilla ice cream.

Food Facts

Strawberries are a good source of vitamin C, which is excellent for your skin, hair, and nails and also helps to boost your immune system.

strawberries

4 Add more sauce and fruit and then top the sundae with a scoop of Yogourt Ice and a sprinkling of nuts. Repeat to make three more sundaes.

Fruity Apple Muffins

Tasty Twists

Instead of the English muffins, try raisin bread, brioche, or currant buns. Alternatively, plain or fruit scones, bagels, pancakes, or waffles taste great!

This recipe is perfect if you are looking to make a simple dessert but don't have much time on your hands. The apples can be peeled first if you prefer, but they are more nutritious with the skin on.

Serve the soft, golden apples on top of the eggy muffins.

Ingredients

- 3 apples
- 10 mL (2 tsp) lemon juice
- 30 mL (2 tbsp) unsalted butter (plus extra for cooking muffins)
- 30 mL (2 tbsp) soft light brown sugar
- 2 mL (½ tsp) ground nutmeg
- 2 eggs (lightly beaten)
- 60 mL (4 tbsp) milk
- 4 cinnamon and raisin English muffins (halved)

English muffins

lighty beaten eggs

Equipment

- small sharp knife
- cutting board
- medium-sized bowl
- wooden spoon
- large frying pan
- foil
- tablespoon
- spatula
- shallow dish

shallow dish

large frying pan

1 Cut the apples into quarters and remove the cores. Cut the apples into thin slices. Put the slices in a bowl and add the lemon juice to coat the apples.

2 Melt the butter in the frying pan and then add the apple slices. Cook over a medium-low heat for 3–4 minutes, stirring frequently.

Food Facts

It's healthier not to peel the apples. Two-thirds of the fibre and lots of antioxidants are found in the skin. Antioxidants help to reduce damage to cells, which can trigger some diseases. Apples aid digestion and are said to be good for skin problems.

apples

3 Add the sugar and nutmeg and cook for another 1–2 minutes, or until the apples have softened and the sauce turns golden and caramelizes.

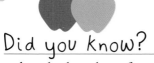

4 Remove the apples from the heat and put them in a bowl. Cover the bowl to keep the apples warm. Set aside while you prepare the muffins.

Did you know?

Charred apples have been found in prehistoric dwellings in Switzerland, showing that humans have been enjoying apples since at least 6500 BCE. Apples were also the favourite fruit of the ancient Greeks and Romans.

5 Put the eggs and milk into a shallow dish and mix them together. One by one, dip both sides of the muffin halves in the egg mixture.

6 Allow any excess egg mixture to drip off the muffins. Then melt a small pat of butter in a frying pan and swirl it around to coat the bottom.

7 Two at a time, put the muffins into the frying pan and cook each side for about 2 minutes or until the egg has set and they are light golden.

Crumbly Cobbler

Cobblers can also be called crumbles, grunts, or slumps. They are easy to make but taste so good they are difficult to resist! Give this traditional dish a healthy twist by adding oats and seeds to the topping.

Tasty Twists

Try different varieties of fruit. Seasonal fruit tends to have the best flavour, so in the summer months you could try nectarines, peaches, plums, or rhubarb, and in late summer/early autumn try apples, blackberries, or pears.

Ingredients

- 4 apples
- 325 mL (1⅓ cup) blueberries (defrosted if frozen)
- 60 mL (4 tbsp) apple juice
- 15 mL (1 tbsp) turbinado sugar

Topping

- 150 mL (⅔ cup) white flour
- 150 mL (⅔ cup) whole wheat flour

- 75 mL (⅓ cup) unsalted butter (cut into small pieces)
- 125 mL (½ cup) turbinado sugar
- 45 mL (3 tbsp) sunflower seeds
- 15 mL (1 tbsp) sesame seeds
- 45 mL (3 tbsp) rolled oats

sunflower seeds

turbinado sugar

Equipment

- large mixing bowl
- small sharp knife
- cutting board
- spoon
- 900-mL (2 pint) ovenproof dish
- small jug

sharp knife

cutting board

mixing bowl

1 Preheat the oven to 180°C (350°F). Put the white flour and whole wheat flour into a large mixing bowl and stir together with a spoon.

2 Add the butter. Rub the butter and flour together with your fingertips until they look like coarse breadcrumbs. Stir in the sugar, seeds, and oats.

3 Remove the skin from the apples and cut them into quarters. Then carefully remove the core and slice the fruit into bite-sized pieces.

You can leave the skin on the apples, if you like—it's very good for you.

4 Put the pieces of apple into an ovenproof dish. Add the blueberries and pour over the apple juice. Sprinkle the sugar evenly over the top.

5 Spoon over the topping in an even layer then put the dish in the oven. Cook for 35 minutes until the top is crisp and beginning to brown.

Food Facts

For such a small fruit, blueberries pack a powerful health punch. According to research, they beat 40 other fruits and vegetables in helping to prevent some diseases! They provide a high concentration of antioxidants, which means they may help to prevent cancer and heart disease. What's more, they may help to fight infections, boost memory, and be anti-aging.

blueberries

Fruit Bread Pudding

This is a quick version of the classic British dessert, summer pudding, which is usually made in a bowl and left overnight to allow the fruit juices to soak into the bread.

Did you know?

The word "companion" comes from the Latin words "com" meaning "with" and "panis" meaning "bread," so it originally meant one with whom bread is shared.

Ingredients

- 8 slices whole wheat bread (preferably slightly stale)
- 600 g (1 lb 5 oz) mixed fresh or frozen berries such as strawberries, blackberries, black currants, and raspberries

stale whole wheat bread

blackberries

- 125 mL (½ cup) water
- 125 mL (½ cup) sugar

medium saucepan

strawberries

Equipment

- cutting board
- medium saucepan
- large cookie cutter or scissors
- bowl
- wooden spoon
- sieve
- large shallow dish
- tablespoon
- spatula

sieve

wooden spoon

1 Cut the bread into your chosen shape using scissors or a large cookie cutter. (Use as much of the bread as possible to avoid waste.)

2 Put all but a handful of the berries, the water, and about two-thirds of the sugar into a saucepan. Stir and then bring to a boil. Reduce the heat.

Food Facts

Bread is a staple food of many European, Middle Eastern, and Indian cultures and is prepared by baking, steaming, or frying dough. There are more than 200 different types of bread but for the healthiest diet, you should try and eat whole wheat varieties which contain more fibre and B vitamins.

Whole wheat bread

3 Simmer the berries gently for about 7 minutes or until the fruit is soft and very juicy. Taste and add the remaining sugar if the fruit is too tart.

4 Strain the juice from the fruit into a bowl. Press the fruit through a sieve into another bowl to make a purée. Throw away the seeds.

Tasty Twists

This delicious fruit purée would also taste great spooned over Banana Pancakes (see p.28-29) or Tropical Yogourt Ice (see p.90-91).

5 Place 4 bread shapes in a large shallow dish and spoon over the fruit purée until the bread is completely covered with the fruit.

6 Add a second piece of bread on top of the first. Spoon over the remaining purée and the berry juice. Gently press the bread with the back of a spoon.

7 Leave for at least 30 minutes to allow the bread to soak up the juice. Carefully lift out of the dish and decorate with the leftover berries and a little juice.

Apple Bars

Preheat the oven to 180°C (350°F). Over a low heat, melt 140 mL (½ cup + 1 tbsp) butter with 250 mL (1 cup) brown sugar and 45 mL (3 tbsp) corn syrup. Put 250 mL (1 cup) oats, 1 apple (cored and grated), and 30 mL (2 tbsp) sunflower seeds into a mixing bowl and stir in the butter mixture. Pour it into a greased 20 cm square cake pan and bake in an oven for 20–25 minutes. Cool; cut into squares.

Baking

Store-bought cakes and cookies are usually high in sugar and fat. Many of the recipes in this section contain fruit whose natural sweetness helps to reduce the amount of refined sugar needed, as well as adding vitamins. Nutritious whole wheat flour is also used to add extra fibre and B vitamins. Here are a few suggestions to get you started.

Apple Tart

Preheat the oven to 180°C (350°F). Cut out 10 cm circles of ready-rolled puff pastry. Arrange thinly sliced apples over the top, leaving a 1 cm gap around the edge. Gently score the pastry around the fruit. Melt a little jam or honey in a small pan and brush it over the top of the apples. Place on a baking sheet and bake for 20–25 minutes, or until the pastry becomes golden.

Oat Bread

Oats are high in fibre and can help lower high cholesterol and blood pressure. Here's how to adapt the roll recipe on p.122–123 to make a loaf of oat bread: Replace 125 mL (½ cup) of the whole wheat bread flour with 75 mL (⅓ cup) oats in step 2. In step 6, make 1 large loaf instead of 10 rolls and sprinkle the loaf with oats before baking it in step 7.

Savoury Scones

Preheat the oven to 220°C (425°F). Sift 250 mL (1 cup) each of whole wheat and white self-rising flour and 2 mL (½ tsp) salt into a bowl. Rub in 50 mL (3½ tbsp) butter until the mixture looks like breadcrumbs. Make a well in the centre and pour in 150 mL (⅔ cup) milk. (If you like add 50 g/2 oz of cheese, sun dried tomatoes, or ham.) Mix to form a sticky dough and turn out onto a floured surface. Knead lightly until the dough is smooth and shape it into a circle about 2.5 cm thick. Cut into smaller circles and brush the tops with milk. Place on a greased baking sheet and bake for about 20 mins.

Open Sandwich

Bread does not have to be made with wheat flour—you could use spelt, rye, corn flour, or buckwheat flour. Try an open sandwich with a new type of bread. Experiment with toppings such as lettuce, cottage cheese, and ham.

Fruity Muffins

Fresh and dried fruit add both sweetness and vitamins to your baking. On p.108–109 you could stir 250 mL (1 cup) of your favourite fruits such as blueberries and raspberries, apples, bananas, or apricots into the mixture in step 4, instead of dates.

Flatbread

This flatbread makes a great sandwich wrap. Put 375 mL (1½ cups) whole wheat self-rising flour and 2 mL (½ tsp) salt into a bowl. Stir in 15 mL (1 tbsp) vegetable oil and 125 mL (½ cup) water to make a soft dough. Knead on a lightly floured surface and put the dough into a lightly oiled bowl. Cover with plastic wrap and leave for 1 hour. Then, divide the dough into 8 pieces and roll each one into circles, about 2 mm thick. Heat a lightly oiled, non-stick frying pan and cook for about 1½ minutes on each side, until golden and puffy.

Seed Rolls

Nuts and seeds give breads, cookies, and cakes a delicious taste and texture, as well as adding important nutrients. For example, in step 3 of the roll recipe on p.122–123, try adding 75 mL (5 tbsp) of chopped nuts and seeds instead of sprinkling sunflower seeds on the top.

Sticky Date Muffins

These muffins taste light and luscious! The secret to good muffins is to not over-beat the batter, otherwise the muffins will be heavy and dense. For the perfect muffins, give the mixture a gentle stir with a wooden spoon until the flour just disappears.

Did you know?

Dates are the fruit of the date palm tree, which can grow up to 25 metres tall. Egypt is the world's largest producer of dates.

Ingredients

sugar

- 400 mL (1⅔ cups) white or whole wheat flour
- 15 mL (1 tbsp) baking powder
- 75 mL (⅓ cup) sugar
- 5 mL (1 tsp) ground cinnamon
- 2 mL (½ tsp) salt
- 75 mL (⅓ cup) dried chopped dates

- 15 mL (1 tbsp) orange juice

egg

- 175 mL (¾ cup) milk
- 1 large egg (lightly beaten)
- 175 mL (¾ cup) butter

ground cinnamon

whole wheat flour

Equipment

blender

- large muffin tin
- paper baking cups
- sieve
- large mixing bowl
- wooden spoon ● fork
- food processor or blender
- small saucepan
- measuring cup
- wire rack

muffin tin

1 Preheat the oven to 200°C (400°F). Line the muffin tin with the paper baking cups. Sift the flour and baking powder into a bowl.

2 Stir the sugar, cinnamon, and salt into the flour and baking powder. Put the dates and orange juice in a blender and whiz until they form a smooth purée.

3 Melt the butter in a saucepan over a low heat. Pour the milk into a measuring cup and add the egg, melted butter, and date purée. Beat together lightly with a fork.

108

Tasty Twists

Fresh fruit such as blueberries, raspberries, and strawberries make a delicious alternative to the puréed dates. Alternatively, try other dried fruits such as raisins, cherries, apricots, cranberries, or prunes.

Food Facts

Dates are one of the oldest cultivated fruits in the world and have been around since about 6000 BCE. They are soft and tasty and a natural sweetener. Dates are also a good source of iron, fibre, and potassium as well as being low in fat.

dates

4 Pour the date mixture into the flour mixture. Fold the ingredients together gently and evenly with a wooden spoon until the flour is just mixed in.

5 Spoon the mixture into the paper cups until it is almost to the top. Bake for 20 minutes until risen and golden. Transfer the muffins to a wire rack to cool.

Passion Cake

With no creaming or whisking, this is a deliciously simple cake recipe. Carrots give the cake a light and moist texture, as well as providing essential nutrients.

Decorate the cake with slivers of orange peel.

Helpful Hints

To test if the cake is cooked, insert a metal skewer into its centre. If it comes out clean, without cake mixture sticking to it, the cake is ready to take out of the oven.

Ingredients

whole wheat self-rising flour

- butter (for greasing)
- 250 mL (1 cup) whole wheat self-rising flour
- 250 mL (1 cup) white self-rising flour
- 10 mL (2 tsp) pumpkin pie spice
- 300 mL (1¼ cups) turbinado sugar

eggs

- 550 mL (2¼ cups) carrots (peeled and grated)
- 4 eggs
- 175 mL (¾ cup) sunflower oil
- 125 mL (½ cup) reduced-fat cream cheese
- 5 mL (1 tsp) vanilla extract
- 75 mL (5 tbsp) icing sugar

Equipment

- 20 cm square cake pan
- parchment paper
- sieve
- large mixing bowl
- wooden spoon
- measuring cup
- skewer
- spatula

measuring cup

sieve

1 Preheat the oven to 180°C (350°F). Lightly grease a 20 cm square cake pan and then carefully line the base with parchment paper.

2 Sift both types of flour into a bowl, adding any bran left in the sieve. Stir in the pumpkin spice, turbinado sugar, and carrots until they are thoroughly combined.

3 Crack the eggs into a measuring cup. Use a fork to lightly beat them together. Then pour the eggs into the bowl with the flour mixture.

4 Add the oil and then stir until all the ingredients are mixed together. Pour the mixture into the pan and smooth the top with the back of a spoon.

Food Facts

Not all fats are unhealthy. Vegetable oil is a type of unsaturated fat which is a good source of energy and helps your body to absorb some vitamins.

Vegetable oil

5 Bake the cake for 50 minutes until it is risen and golden. Remove it from the oven and leave to cool in the pan for 10 minutes before turning it out.

6 Turn the cake out on to a cooling rack. Put the cream cheese and icing sugar into a bowl and beat together until smooth and creamy.

7 Stir in the vanilla extract. Put the icing in the fridge for 15 minutes to harden slightly. Spread the icing over the cake and smooth using a spatula.

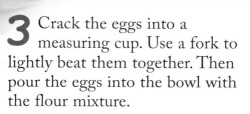

Fruity Oat Bars

Most bar cookies are healthier than many other desserts because they contain oats. This version is extra good for you because of the fruity layer in the middle.

Did you know?

In the UK, the bar cookies are called "flapjacks." No one is really sure from where the word originates, although it does appear in Shakespeare's play *Pericles* from the early 17th century.

Ingredients

- 250 mL (1 cup) dried apricots
- 30 mL (2 tbsp) water
- 552 mL (2⅓) whole wheat flour
- 250 mL (1 cup) oats
- 2 mL (½ tsp) salt
- 425 mL (1¾) sticks unsalted butter
- 175 mL (¾ cup) turbinado sugar
- 30 mL (2 tbsp) light corn syrup

turbinado sugar

unsalted butter

light corn syrup

Equipment

- scissors
- food processor or blender
- tablespoon
- large mixing bowl
- wooden spoon
- medium saucepan
- 18 cm square cake pan
- parchment paper
- spatula

spatula

square cake pan

scissors

Food Facts

Both oats and dried apricots are high in soluble fibre, which helps to control blood sugar levels and keep energy levels steady. Dried apricots are also a good source of stamina-boosting iron.

oats

dried apricots

1 Preheat the oven to 200°C (400°F). Grease and line the bottom of the cake pan with parchment paper. Add the apricots and water to a blender.

2 Process the apricots until they are a purée. Set aside. Put the flour, oats, and salt in a mixing bowl and stir with a wooden spoon until combined.

Tasty Twists

You could use fresh fruit purée instead of dried. Raspberries, plums, blueberries, and blackberries would all taste great. (See p.86.)

3 Melt the butter, sugar, and syrup in a saucepan over a low heat. Stir the mixture occasionally until the butter has completely melted.

4 Pour the butter mixture into the mixing bowl containing the flour, oats, and sugar. Stir until everything is combined in a sticky, oaty mixture.

5 Press half of the mixture into the bottom of the cake pan and smooth it to make an an even layer. Carefully spread the apricot purée over the oaty layer.

6 Press the rest of the oaty mixture over the apricot purée until it is covered. Bake for 25–30 minutes or until the oats are golden on top.

7 Remove from the oven and leave to cool for 5 minutes. Divide the bars into squares and leave them to cool completely in the pan before scooping them out.

Fruit and Nut Cookies

These yummy cookies are full of energy-boosting ingredients such as oats, dried fruit, and nuts. They are much healthier than store-bought ones, and taste better too!

> ⚠️ Nut allergy sufferers should leave out the nuts. The recipe will work just as well without them.

Ingredients

cranberries

- 125 mL (½ cup) dried apricots
- 175 mL (¾ cup) flour (whole wheat or white)
- 175 mL (¾ cup) whole oats
- 125 mL (½ cup) chopped hazelnuts (optional)
- 140 mL (½ cup + 1 tbsp) unsalted butter
- 75 mL (⅓ cup) soft light brown sugar
- 30 mL (2 tbsp) runny honey
- 1 EGGE

 apricots

 honey

 raisins

Equipment

- 2 baking sheets
- scissors
- mixing bowl
- wooden spoon
- sharp knife
- small saucepan
- spoon
- cooling rack

 scissors

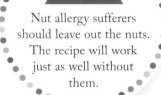

1 Preheat the oven to 180°C (350°F) and lightly grease 2 baking sheets with butter. Cut the apricots into small pieces and put them in a mixing bowl.

2 Add the flour, oats, and nuts to the bowl. Mix together with a wooden spoon. Cut the butter into small chunks and put into a saucepan.

3 Add the sugar and honey to the saucepan. Heat them over a low heat. Stir gently with a wooden spoon, until the butter and sugar have melted.

4 Add the butter mixture to the bowl and mix. Put 5 spoonfuls of the cookie dough onto each baking sheet, leaving space between each one.

5 Flatten the cookies a little so they are about 5 cm diameter and 1 cm thick. Bake for 15 minutes or until they are light golden.

Tasty Twists

Chopped dried cherries, raisins, cranberries, peaches or dates can be used instead of apricots and any other nuts, such as walnuts or pecans, can be used instead of hazelnuts.

6 Remove the baking sheets from the oven and leave the cookies to cool slightly. Then transfer the cookies to a cooling rack to cool and become crisp.

Food Facts

Flour is made by grinding grain, usually wheat. Whole wheat flour is made from the whole wheat grain with nothing added or taken away. It is higher in fibre and B vitamins than white flour, which is refined and processed until only about 75% of the grain is left. B vitamins are essential for producing energy, while fibre helps your digestive system work more efficiently.

wheat

Cherry and Apple Pies

Cherries and apples are combined in this variation of a classic dessert. This type of pie is called a free-form pie because it is not cooked in a dish and the sides of the pastry are simply gathered up to encase the filling.

Helpful Hint

Ground almonds, semolina, or fine polenta help to soak up the fruit juices and prevent the pastry from getting soggy. Ground almonds also add extra flavour, but nut allergy sufferers should use semolina or fine polenta instead.

Ingredients

- 75 mL (⅓ cup) unsalted butter (plus extra to glaze)
- 30 mL (2 tbsp) sugar
- 1 large egg (lightly beaten)
- 425 mL (1¾ cups) flour (plus extra for dusting)
- 15 mL (1 tbsp) water

Filling

- 30 mL (2 tbsp) sugar
- 395 mL (1⅓ cups) pitted cherries (fresh or canned)
- 2 apples
- 75 mL (⅓ cup) ground almonds, semolina, or fine polenta

Glaze

- 1 large egg (lightly beaten)

apples

Equipment

- 2 large baking sheets
- baking paper
- scissors
- mixing bowl
- food processor or blender
- plastic wrap
- sieve
- vegetable peeler
- rolling pin

plastic wrap

food processor

Did you know?

Cherries date back to the Stone Age. Cherry pits have been found in many Stone Age caves in Europe.

1 Line the baking sheets. Put the butter, 75 mL (⅓ cup) of sugar, and 1 egg into a food processor and process until smooth and creamy.

2 Add the flour and 15 mL (1 tbsp) of water to the processor and whiz until the mixture comes together in a ball. The pastry will be quite soft.

Food Facts

Canned fruit can be used in this recipe when cherries are not in season, such as during the winter months. Choose fruit canned in natural juices rather than with added sugar or syrup.

canned cherries

3 Turn the dough out on to a lightly floured work surface and gather it until it forms a smooth ball. Cover with plastic wrap and chill for 30 minutes.

4 Preheat the oven to 200°C (400°F). While the pastry is chilling, drain the cherries in a sieve (if using canned) and mix with the apples, sugar, and almonds.

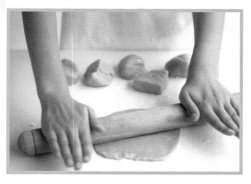

5 Divide the pastry into 6 pieces. On a lightly floured surface, roll the pastry into thin circles about 13 cm in diameter. Put on the baking sheet.

6 Brush the pastry with egg and sprinkle on the almonds. Add the fruit, leaving a 2.5 cm border. Gently gather the pastry to make open-topped pies.

7 Brush the outside of the pies with egg. Place a small piece of butter on top of the fruit. Bake the pies for 25 mins or until the pastry is light golden.

Raisin Soda Bread

Soda bread is the perfect starting point for anyone who hasn't made bread before. It doesn't contain yeast so it doesn't need as much kneading or rising as ordinary bread, but it's just as tasty.

If the dough is too dry in step 4, add a little extra buttermilk.

Helpful Hints

If you can't find buttermilk in the store, use the same quantity of low-fat plain yogourt or milk combined with 15 mL (1 tbsp) of lemon juice.

Ingredients

- 395 mL (1⅓ cup) whole wheat flour
- 395 mL (1⅓ cup) white flour (plus extra for dusting)
- 5 mL (1 tsp) salt
- 5 mL (1 tsp) baking soda
- 150 mL (⅔ cup) oats
- 15–17 mL (1 heaped tbsp) sugar
- 250 mL (1 cup) raisins
- 1 egg (lightly beaten)
- 300–375ml (1¼–1½ cups) buttermilk or plain yogourt

raisins

whole wheat flour

Equipment

- baking sheet
- sieve
- measuring cup
- large mixing bowl
- wooden spoon
- knife

wooden spoon

large mixing bowl

Food Facts

Traditionally, buttermilk is the liquid remaining after the cream has been churned into butter. It is low in fat and is often used to make pancakes and scones as well as soda bread. When combined with baking soda, it acts as a raising agent. Remember, if you can't find buttermilk, plain yogourt is a great alternative.

buttermilk

Tasty Twists

Chopped dried dates, cranberries, blueberries, or cherries could be used instead of raisins—or you could try a mixture of dried fruits.

1 Preheat the oven to 200°C (400°F). Sprinkle a baking sheet with flour until it is lightly covered. This will prevent the loaf sticking to the sheet.

2 Sift the whole wheat and white flour, salt, and baking soda into a mixing bowl. If there is any bran left in the sieve, add it to the bowl.

3 Add oats, sugar, and raisins to the bowl and stir. Make a well in the centre of the mixture and pour in the egg and 300 mL (1¼ cups) of the buttermilk.

4 Mix together with a wooden spoon. When the mixture starts to come together, use your hands to form a soft, slightly sticky ball of dough.

5 Put the dough onto a lightly floured work surface and gently knead, once or twice, until the dough is smooth. Don't over-knead or the dough will toughen.

6 Form the dough into a flattish circle, about 18 cm in diameter and 4 cm thick. Put the dough on the floured baking sheet.

7 Sift over a little extra flour. Cut a large, deep cross, almost to the bottom of the dough. Bake for 30–35 minutes, or until risen and golden.

Banana and Pineapple Cake

This rich, moist cake is the tastiest loaf around! It is the perfect addition to a picnic or school lunchbox or it makes a great after dinner treat.

Did you know?

Banana plants have been around for a long time. One of the first records dates back to Alexander the Great's conquest of India—where he first discovered bananas in 327 BCE!

Ingredients

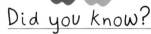
self-rising whole wheat flour

bananas

- 125 mL (½ cup) unsalted butter, cut into small pieces (plus extra for greasing)
- 5 small bananas (about 450 g/1 lb peeled weight)
- 125 mL (½ cup) dried pineapple
- 325 mL (1⅓ cups) self-rising white flour
- 125 mL (½ cup) self-rising whole wheat flour
- 5 mL (1 tsp) baking powder
- pinch of salt
- 150 mL (⅔ cup) sugar
- 2 large eggs
- 75 mL (⅓ cup) chopped walnuts (optional)

eggs

Equipment

scissors

mixing bowl

- large loaf pan
- parchment paper
- small bowl
- fork
- scissors
- sieve
- large mixing bowl
- wooden spoon

loaf pan

1 Preheat the oven to 180°C (350°F). Trace around the loaf pan onto parchment paper and cut it out. Lightly grease the pan with butter and then line.

2 Put the bananas in a bowl and mash them with a fork. Cut the pineapple into very small pieces. Set the bananas and pineapple aside.

Helpful Hint

If you can't find self-rising flour, use all-purpose flour, but add 2 mL (½ tsp) salt and 7 mL (½ tbsp) baking powder for every 250 mL (1 cup) of flour.

3 Sift the flour, baking powder, and salt into a mixing bowl. Stir and then add the butter. Rub the butter into the flour mixture until it looks like fine breadcrumbs.

4 One at a time, crack the eggs into a small bowl. Lightly beat the eggs together with a fork until the whites and yolks are mixed together.

Food Facts

Pineapple is great for a sensitive stomach because it contains an enzyme called bromelain which is anti-inflammatory. It helps to reduce swelling and aids speedy recovery from surgery. It also aids digestion.

pineapple

5 Pour the beaten eggs into the mixing bowl, add the sugar, bananas, and pineapple and mix together. Pour the cake mixture into the prepared loaf pan.

6 Make sure the mixture is level and then sprinkle over the walnuts. Cook in the centre of the oven for about 50 minutes until risen and golden.

7 Remove from the oven and place on a cooling rack for 10 minutes. Carefully turn the cooled cake out of the tin, cut into slices, and serve.

Sunflower Seed Rolls

There's nothing like the aroma of fresh bread! All you need is a handful of basic ingredients to make these seedy rolls. You could also make a single loaf instead of the rolls (see p.106).

(see p.106)

Tasty Twists

Bread flour is a high-protein flour that helps dough rise and makes bread lighter and fluffier. You can use all-purpose flour as well, but the result will be a denser bread.

To test if the rolls are cooked, lightly tap the base—if it sounds hollow, it is cooked!

Ingredients

- 375 mL (1½ cups) lukewarm water
- 10 mL (2 tsp) dried yeast
- 625 mL (2½ cups) white bread flour
- 375 mL (1½ cups) whole wheat bread flour
- 7 mL (1½ tsp) salt
- 1 egg (beaten)
- 75 mL (5 tbsp) sunflower seeds

sunflower seeds

whole wheat bread flour

Equipment

- small bowl
- large mixing bowl
- wooden spoon or tablespoon
- measuring cup
- baking sheets
- pastry brush

mixing bowl

wooden spoon

1 Pour 125 mL (½ cup) of lukewarm water into a small bowl. Sprinkle in the yeast and stir gently until dissolved. Set the yeast aside for 5 minutes, to activate.

2 Put both types of flour and the salt into a large mixing bowl and mix together. Make a well (a large hole) in the centre of the flour.

3 Pour the yeast and most of the remaining water into the well and gently stir in the flour. Stir in the rest of the water, if necessary, to make a soft dough.

4 Turn the dough out on to a floured work surface. Knead for 10 minutes until smooth and shiny. Put the dough in a clean bowl and cover with a tea towel.

5 Leave to rise for 1½–2 hours, until it has doubled in size. Preheat the oven to 220°C (425°F). Punch down the risen dough with your knuckles.

6 Divide the dough into 10 pieces. Dust your hands with flour and shape the dough into rolls. Cover the rolls and set aside for 10 minutes.

7 Brush each roll with beaten egg and gently press the sunflower seeds into the tops. Bake for 25–30 minutes or until risen and golden.

Food Facts

Yeast is a single-celled micro-organism that is part of the fungus family and can be bought fresh or dried. It is used in bread-making to make the dough rise and give the bread a light, airy texture. To work, the yeast needs warmth and moisture. It ferments and produces tiny bubbles of gas which make the dough rise and give it a light, spongy texture.

fresh yeast

Glossary

This is the place to find extra information about the cooking words and techniques used in this book.

A

Additives: substances added to processed food to add colour, flavour, or extend its shelf life.

Amino acids: proteins known as the "building blocks of life" because they are necessary for the body to grow and repair itself. The body can make some itself, but others are obtained from food.

Antibodies: proteins made by the body's immune system to fight viruses or bacteria.

Anti-inflammatory: a property of a substance that reduces signs of inflammation such as swelling, heat, redness, and pain.

Antioxidant: vitamins, minerals, and phytochemicals that protect the body against the damaging effects of too many free radicals (which can damage the body's cells).

B

B Vitamins: a group of vitamins essential for the breakdown of carbohydrates, proteins, and fats in the body. They are thiamin, riboflavin, niacin, B6, pantothenic acid, biotin, folic acid, and B12.

Bake: to cook food in an oven. This uses dry heat (without liquid) and browns the outside of the food.

Beat: to stir or mix an ingredient quickly, to add air.

Beneficial bacteria: bacteria living in the intestines that that help to break down food and keep harmful bacteria from multiplying.

Beta carotene: the substance that gives orange and yellow fruit and vegetables their colour. It is converted by the body into vitamin A.

Bioflavonoids: compounds found in fruit and sweet vegetables. They help to maintain the health of blood capillaries.

Bland: describes food which has little flavour of its own.

Blend: to mix ingredients together by hand or in a blender or food processor to form a liquid or smooth mixture.

Blood sugar levels: the amount of sugar (glucose) in the blood. Bad diet can make this level rise and fall too quickly, causing health problems such as dizziness and mood swings.

Boil: to heat a liquid to a very hot temperature so that it bubbles and gives off steam.

Bran: husks of cereal grains that have been separated from the flour.

Broil: to cook or brown food under intense heat.

Brown: to cook food, usually by baking, frying, broiling, or grilling, so that it becomes golden.

C

Calcium: a mineral essential for healthy bones and teeth. It also helps muscles and nerves to work properly.

Carbohydrates: the sugars, fibres, and starches that are found in fruits, vegetables, grains, and milk products. They are used by the body as a source of energy.

Carotenoids: pigments similar to carotene found in some plant foods.

Cholesterol: a fat mainly produced in the liver. Diets rich in saturated fats may lead to high cholesterol levels in the blood, increasing the risk of heart attacks and strokes.

Concentrated: when food has had non-essential ingredients, such as water, removed.

Cultivation: preparing soil for growing crops by digging it and removing weeds.

D

Deep-fry: to fry in a deep pan with a lot of oil so that the food becomes golden and crispy.

Digestion: the process by which the body breaks down foods that have been eaten so that they can be used for essential functions such as growth and repair.

Digestive system: the organs of the body through which food passes as it is being digested. They are the mouth, esophagus, stomach, and intestines. The liver and pancreas are also part of the digestive system as they secrete chemicals necessary for digestion.

Dough: a firm mixture of flour, liquid, and usually other ingredients, that can be kneaded and shaped to make bread, rolls, or pastry.

Dry fry: to fry without oil or fat.

E

Enzymes: proteins made from amino acids that set off chemical reactions in the body. Each enzyme has a specific function; for example, lactase is an enzyme whose only function is to break down lactose in milk products.

F

Fats: food group that includes oils and hard fats such as butter. Fats may be either saturated or unsaturated. Too many saturated fats can cause heart disease, whereas unsaturated fats generally help to prevent it.

Fatty acids: the main part of all fats—for example saturated, polyunsaturated, and monounsaturated. The wrong balance of fatty acids can increase the risk of heart disease.

Fibre: the part of a plant food that is not digested, but passes through the digestive system and out of the body. Fibre is good for you because it helps to keep your bowels working properly.

Free-range: a word to describe farm animals that have been bred and kept in conditions where they are free to move around. It also describes the eggs of free-range hens.

Fry: to cook food over a direct heat in a frying pan or saucepan, using a little oil.

G

Germ: a tiny organism, only visible under a microscope, that is capable of invading the body and causing disease. Bacteria and viruses are germs.

Griddle: to cook food over heat on a special ridged pan that allows the fat to run away.

Grill: to cook or brown food over intense heat.

H

Husk: the outer covering of a seed or grain.

I

Immune system: the body's self-defense system, whose job is to fight infection and disease.

Iron: a mineral the body needs to make healthy red blood cells. If you don't get enough iron in your diet, your blood will not be able to deliver oxygen to your body efficiently.

K

Knead: to fold and press dough with your hands to make it smooth and stretchy. This strengthens the gluten (a protein) in the flour.

L

Lean: meat that is composed mainly of muscle, containing little fat.

Lycopene: an antioxidant vitamin that is plentiful in tomatoes and some other red-coloured fruits and vegetables, such as watermelon.

M

Magnesium: a mineral needed for many vital body functions. It helps to regulate the heartbeat, strengthen bones and maintain nerve function.

Marinade: usually a mixture of oil and other flavourings that meat, fish, or vegetables may be soaked in before cooking.

Marinate: to soak meat, fish, or vegetables in the above before cooking so that they absorb flavour and stay moist and tender.

Melt: to reduce a solid, such as butter, to a liquid using heat.

Micro-organism: an organism so small it can only be seen under a microscope.

Minerals: nutrients found in food that are essential to keep the body healthy. They are only needed in small amounts.

N

Nutrients: compounds contained within food that provide nourishment to the body. They include proteins, carbohydrates, fats, vitamins, and minerals.

P

Phosphorus: an essential mineral that helps the cells in your body to function normally.

Phytochemicals: chemicals which come from plants. They are not strictly nutrients but they help your body to fight diseases and stay healthy.

Poach : to cook in gently simmering liquid, especially eggs and fish.

Potassium: a mineral that is essential for growth and good health. Among other things it keeps your blood pressure normal and helps your muscles to work properly.

Protein: this comes from both plant and animal sources and helps your body to grow and stay healthy. Protein is made up of small components called amino acids.

Pureé: fruits, vegetables, legumes, meat, or fish that are blended or liquidized (usually with liquid) to make a pulp.

R

Raising agent: a substance such as baking powder used to add air or gas to make food rise and become light and fluffy.

Refined: food that has been processed. Whole-grain foods are better for you because they have not been overly refined.

Roast: to cook food in the oven at a high temperature.

S

Sauté: to fry using oil or fat to brown food.

Season: to add salt and pepper to food to add flavour and bring out other flavours.

Selenium: a mineral that helps your immune system. It is also an antioxidant which protects your cells.

Shred: to cut or tear food into narrow strips.

Sift: to put food through a mesh utensil called a sieve in order to remove lumps or coarse particles.

Slice: to cut food into thin or thick pieces, using a knife.

Staple food: the food which forms the main part of a community's diet. It is usually a carbohydrate food such as rice or potatoes.

Stir: to mix food in a circular motion, usually with a spoon.

Stir-fry: to fry food in a little oil over a high heat, stirring constantly.

T

Toast: to brown or crisp food, especially bread, using a toaster, grill, or frying pan.

Toxin: a substance that has a negative effect on your body. It can enter your body in or on what you eat.

V

Vitamin A: also known as retinol, this vitamin helps maintain the health of your skin. It also strengthens immunity from infections and helps vision in dim light.

Vitamin C: also known as ascorbic acid, this vitamin protects your cells and helps your body to absorb iron from food.

Vitamin D: this helps to regulate the amount of calcium and phosphorus in your body.

Vitamin E: an antioxidant that helps protect cell membranes.

Vitamins: essential nutrients that your body needs to work properly and stay healthy.

W

Whisk: to briskly mix ingredients together using a fork or whisk in order to combine them and add air.

Z

Zinc: an element that helps your body to make new cells and enzymes. It also processes protein, fat, and carbohydrates and helps to heal wounds.

Index

Bold entries indicate a recipe.